M000305872

The Outnation

A Search for the Soul of Japan

JONATHAN RAUCH

The Outnation
A Search for the Soul of Japan

FOREWORD BY DREUX RICHARD

Acorn Abbey

Copyright © 1992, 2021 Jonathan Rauch

Published 2021 by Acorn Abbey Books

Madison, North Carolina

All rights reserved

ISBN 978-1-949450-03-3

New edition with a new foreword by Dreux Richard

First published 1992, Harvard Business School Press

Author's note

I wrote *The Outnation* in 1990 and 1991 and published it in 1992, a very different time in Japan's history than today. The so-called bubble economy had only just peaked; although no one yet knew it, a long period of economic stagnation would ensue, bringing with it a multitude of social changes, including a loosening of some of the tight social strictures I describe in this book. Almost 30 years later, Japan is in many ways a different place. A visitor to Tokyo will find it much more legible to foreigners than the Japan I explored three decades ago—more westernized, in ways both superficial and deep. The exotic, opaque, and sometimes even sinister qualities reported by foreigners in the 1980s and early 1990s are much less in evidence. Perhaps more important, nowadays no one is afraid of Japan. The obsessive gaze of the West, and also of Japan itself, has shifted to China, today's problematic "outnation," which seems and certainly is more problematic than Japan.

Still, as I reread *The Outnation* with the three decades' perspective, I find that its larger social and political observations still hold. The sublimation of conflict, the difficulties choosing an agenda, the quiet rebellions of the young, the machine-style politics, the fatalism about decline, the sense of being a "small island nation" despite its economic strength: all of that, and much more, still obtains. And so I have chosen to republish the original text unchanged.

In this new edition I have not been able to include the original's photos by Joel Sackett, which so enriched the first publication by the Harvard Business School Press. James Fallows's original foreword has been replaced with a new one by Dreux Richard, a gifted writer who represents a new generation of reportorial talent. It is reassuring to know that discerning young eyes continue to focus on Japan and see below its surfaces, as Richard does so memorably in his book, *Every Human Intention: Japan in the New Century*; it is an honor to have him present mine.

Jonathan Rauch, Fairfax County, Virginia, July 2021

The Orphan and the Elephant

—foreword by Dreux Richard

Japan allegedly was the birthplace of the internet comment, originally appended to online news stories by a Scottish couple who maintained a popular website for English-speaking expatriates. The average expatriate, they observed, knew more about Japan than the foreign correspondents who periodically cycled through, and enjoyed making their superior comprehension known; why not allow them to do it on the pages where stories appeared?

In the comments sections, the most caustic critiques were reserved for veteran journalists who seeded Japan's hothouse of stereotypes (East meets West, feudal meets ultramodern, neon-lit vice meets white-collar punctiliousness). Decades of cultivated skepticism were apparently no match for a first encounter with a capsule hotel or Tokyo's clean and efficient subway system.

As a remedy for the credulous habits of foreign journalists, the internet comment has been unsuccessful. In 2019, Japan's alluring stereotypes claimed their most prestigious victim—the fact checking department of *The New Yorker*. An award-winning author the magazine sent to Japan was duped by a handful of amateur thespians into believing that she had unlimited access to the most successful firm in Japan's "rental family" business. As it turns out, that business barely exists, and the firm in question was fictitious.

This author—one of my generation's best—never had a chance, and neither did her fact checkers. The *arrival narrative*, so ubiquitous in writing about Japan, is best practiced by people who choose to stay in the country, reflecting on their initial experiences after many years have passed. The true arrival story, written by someone who visited Japan briefly and has no other story to tell, is more volume than mass, a slender beam of insight propping up a façade of unfinished impressions.

Exceptions exist, and you can recognize them by the quality of their metaphors. David Rakoff spent less than four months in Tokyo in 1986, and fifteen years later wrote "Tokyo Story," an essay that ends on the sound of a few chocolate-covered almonds rattling in their carton. The almonds are a staple of Japan's subway kiosks and vending machines. Anyone who has worked in Tokyo will recognize the poignant absurdity of feeling somehow *cared for* by the world's largest metropolis because, at the end of a long day, a box of candy always seems to last longer than you thought it would, soothing the very sources of exhaustion responsible for the torpid pace of your eating. Rakoff made Japan as real in his prose as it was in his brief experience there.

I've only read one book about Japan that succeeds as an arrival narrative, and it's the book that begins when this foreword ends. Like Rakoff, Jonathan Rauch arrived in bubble-era Japan as a young, gay, atheist Jew—accustomed to observing the world from slightly outside it—and stayed for less than a year. In that time, he discovered that "the Japanese are precisely as mysterious and unique as my aunt in Hackensack." This argument is directed at many of the books that preceded his, specifically their promise to unravel Japan's national enigmas. Where these enigmas supposedly dwelled, Rauch encountered only the cultural property that every nation possesses: a homeland, a history, and a set of institutions that reflect the will of the public, but only after distorting it. You can experience enough of Japan during the course of a few months, he learned, to overcome your confusion, your sense of romance, and finally to discard that most pathological strain of commentary thought—the desire to reach an elegant conclusion.

The beginner's mind is not always a disadvantage for visitors to Japan. The two best-known expatriate intellectuals to reside in the country remained deliberately illiterate. Rather than repeat the patterns of certainty that connected them to their native cultures, they positioned themselves outside the scope of Japan's prejudices, in a place where they were certain to become living extensions of the people they came to know—communities chosen and refined as an act of literary creativity, rather than biological and social inheritance.

Jonathan Rauch orphaned himself in just this way. He was soon introduced to Donald Richie, the central figure of Japan's expatriate literary tradition. Among the many fortunate results is the structure of this book, which reads like a Japanese novel in its customary, serialized form (Japan's great novels were first published in newspapers). Rauch subsequently met the brilliant journalists and bureaucrats who chose to operate on the fringes of Japan's bubble-era institutions, people who immediately pointed out that only Japan's economy was world-class; its universities, its judicial system, and its democracy—its system of producing and refining notions—were conspicuously second-rate. One doesn't meet these people by going to Japan armored in his American agenda. They belong to a club whose motto is the same in every country: The less you look for, the more you'll find.

Rauch found his best material without looking. One of his interview subjects shared a vivid memory of a bored policeman writing 天皇 (Emperor) on the foggy glass of his sentry booth, then snapping to attention—with visible embarrassment—when he realized he was being observed.

By the time Rauch heard this story, the Emperor had died, prompting an anguished debate about his responsibility for World War II. Fond attachment to his reign could only be found in the nostalgic doodles of minor authority figures. Presumably, the policeman was once like the rowdy, cheerful elementary school students Rauch observed in Niigata, exhilarated by the difference between right and wrong answers—their first unequivocal relationship with truth. What happens in the years between, in a society where "the crushing of curiosity is a side effect, not a goal," Rauch neither criticizes nor admires in *The Outnation*. He yearns to develop a view of his environment that acknowledges its vastness.

He does not, in the process, abandon his faculties as a journalist and political economist. Japan's asset bubble was a nervous, wobbling hulk by the time Rauch saw it in person. It would soon reveal itself as a prolonged exercise in wishful thinking. Most authors who had written about the bubble were instantly discredited for taking its achievements seriously. Dissenters and skeptics suddenly appeared clairvoyant, but even their approach was too consumed by the notions they claimed to criticize. In Rauch's account, the bubble was neither a pyramid scheme nor a model of inspired policy-making. It was "Mexico with an efficient bureaucracy"—cartel capitalism in a self-perfecting state of fermentation. Thirty years after the bubble, *The Outnation* is the only book that navigates the bubble without inflating its significance, or wrongly identifying it as a report card for Japanese culture's broader coherence.

The only "bubble book" still worth reading; the only arrival narrative that succeeds in the form of a book—these may seem like distinctions that matter only if you're disposed to making detailed comparisons between books about Japan written by foreigners. But bubble-era Japan was a global project, the nation that emerged from our atomic leap into an era of borderless catastrophes. Writers and thinkers visited Japan's growing cities in an attempt to glimpse the world's future. The scene was distinctly American, and whenever the country is explained to American readers in exotic terms, the resulting inaccuracies (as Rauch points out) result from the author's "failing to look our own country in the eye." Readers attuned to the illusions and shortcomings of their own cultures will recognize them in the gaze that Rauch casts on Japan.

Like Donald Richie before him, Rauch savored the moments when the behavior he observed around him expressed Japan's innermost contradictions—when he was able to "touch the elephant." I am reminded of the time when I lived in the city of Aba, an industrial hub in southeastern Nigeria destroyed during that nation's civil war. The city's recovery was self-consciously modeled after post-war Japan, and Aba's leaders proudly called it "the Japan of Africa." Its native name is *Enyimba*, or literally "the elephant belongs to the people." In Aba and Japan alike, one senses the presence of the economy as if it were a physical, living entity. It dines with you, listens to you, sleeps outside your window; it leads you to obstacles or clears them from your path, determining the people you meet and places you stay. You discover that its pace naturally matches yours—or have you matched yourself to it? Eventually it changes shape, and no experience is more disorienting than reaching into the empty space it once occupied.

To make sense of this experience, you seek out the person who watched the transformation take place. Turn the page and you'll find him.

Dreux Richard, New Haven, Connecticut, July 2021

Part One

1

We are all feeling the elephant. We are like the blind men in the fable, one touching the trunk, another the tail, another the leg, saying snake or vine or tree; except that we all have our eyes wide open, staring and intent, so that perhaps we are looking too hard; and there are far more of us than three. For foreigners in general, and especially for Americans, Japan presents itself as a singularity in need of explanation. I have been, for example, to Israel, a country whose culture is as unique and strange as any on God's crazy planet, but I felt content to watch and sometimes to laugh or shake my head. I felt no compulsion to explain. Japan is no more singular than that, it is no more strange, but we who come here see it as a knot to be untied, a puzzle to be solved; and so we go to work, each putting a hand out to touch, each looking for the whole within which the parts make sense. Of course, as is always the case, no two of us who examine the beast see quite the same thing or look in the same way; but whereas usually we blame ourselves for this and name as culprit the vagaries of human understanding, in the case of Japan we blame the elephant, and call it a mystery. We insist that something there is in the shadows of Kyoto's gardens or in the dim alleys of Tokyo after hours or in the obscure windings of the Diet's deliberations that remains dark, a mystery.

2

We have been mystified by Japan for at least a century, but at no time has our mystification run deeper or mattered more than now. Japan is one of the great powers, after years of merely promising that it would be. It has become, depending on which patch of the elephant you touch, a threat to other nations or an example to them, a challenge to the so-called "Western" way or a reaffirmation of the Protestant work ethic, of the Jewish commitment to education, of the strong Catholic family. We used to come to Japan because it was exotic; now we come because it is exotic and important; and indeed we are coming. We are here in droves now, all looking for the "real" Japan. Is it "really" a democracy, or is it something else, a regime built on hidden coercion and enforced conformity? Is it really capitalism, is it really a market economy, or is it something new, a third way between Adam Smith and Karl Marx? Is Japan free? Is it benign? Or is it dangerous?

3

Sometimes I fear that, in the din and the crush that we foreigners make, we see and touch mostly each other. I stayed only six months in Japan, but there were moments when I felt that every American intellectual was either in Japan or at home writing about it. For the first time, interest in the beast's anatomy and internal systems has moved outside the circle of professors and diplomats who specialize, and into the reading public; and there, the specialists fear, as they look at the recent spatelet of books and articles creating a small but respectable commotion ("The Coming War with Japan"!), the discussion is getting out of control. Well, out of control is just the way it ought to be. Japan is a major power, and the old relationship with the United States has become suffocating for both parties, and this means we will have to reassess Japan—not as an exotic island on the edge of the world, but as a large and powerful country. And the "we" no longer means "we specialists"; it means you and me, the citizens and voters and businesspeople who must learn how to believe and feel about the place. And so in Japan I put out my hand to touch the elephant and I tried to learn how I ought to feel. I came away knowing only how I ought not to feel.

4

I was, and am, a product of the Arizona desert who moved to the East Coast and cosmopolitanized himself, a timid creature who preferred thinking to doing and who had never before lived abroad, a puzzle solver, a professional outsider, a "Washington journalist" yearning to be free. Washington used to be an exciting and important place. But the world is much bigger than before, and governments generally are less able to exert control. Everyone in Washington feels the blood draining from the governmental center and the capital growing numb and stiff. In any case, I felt it. Like many journalists, I am incorrigibly a generalist, but to the extent that I "am" anything, it is a writer on what has been called political economy, the crossflows of money and power. Nowadays if one wants to understand the flow of money or power or even people, one must confront Asia—Japan especially.

5

Also, I wanted an answer. Anyone who reads about Japan is likely to have noticed that there are the people who have been branded "Japan bashers" (an invidious expression) and the ones who have been branded "Japan handlers" (also invidious), and you can barely believe they are talking about the same place. Japan is big and powerful and unstoppable and incapable of any but the most technical sort of finesse; it gobbles up foreign markets implacably, it earns mountains of cash, it grows and grows. (What *does* it want?) But it is also small and vulnerable and hesitant and delicate; it is peaceloving and eager to please; its people are gentle and want nothing more than to get along with each other and to be liked abroad. There are two prevalent pictures, and they aren't consistent. Yet both seem truthful. Something is wrong. Isn't it?

6

Is there a mystery in Japan? Or are we just confused? Well, if not a mystery, then a sort of puzzle, like a series of numbers that sum one way when added from the top, another way when added from the bottom. Impossible, but there you are. One night a university student in Niigata tells me that he does not want to go to work for one of the big corporations, but it can't be helped. He says he went to New York and loved it—felt free there, does not feel free in Japan. Strange, though: he is not exactly complaining; he is matter-of-fact and placid. The truth is that in today's Japan he could change his fate if he tried, but he won't try. What does one say about this young man, who has chosen not to choose? Free or oppressed? He himself will not say, and in any case he is no judge. What about the business networks (*keiretsu*)—ruthless cartels or beneficent mutualism? The government bureaucracies—fragmented and rivalrous to the point of collective irrationality, or suave and efficient beyond an American bureaucrat's dreams? When Japan is experienced from within, it is calming rather than threatening. Experienced from without, it is a juggernaut.

7

I have an idea how to reconcile the two pictures of Japan. In this first part of the book I'll try to reach it. I want to begin, however, by describing the place: how it looks, how it feels. That is perhaps the best inoculation against the excesses of generalization that I am sure to commit.

8

From far away there is "Japan." It is discrete, unitary, has goals and intentions and methods. In the newspapers it is often spoken of as a person: "Japan" is beating American companies and buying Rockefeller Center, "Japan" will stop buying U.S. government securities, "Japan" believes that economic power is the key to national strength, "Japan" feels shame but not guilt for its wartime misdeeds, "Japan" does this and "Japan" thinks that. This is a natural way to talk, but treacherous. There is, after all, no "Japan." Enter Japan and almost immediately "Japan" disaggregates. A million pieces fall out of the bottom of the box. What you see around you is a blooming, buzzing confusion. There is the national government, but it is composed of jostling factions and feuding ministries, which agree on little and which don't run the country anyway (though they try). There is the business sector, but it is composed of companies of every conceivable size and strength and mission. For every great Mitsubishi or Hitachi there are a thousand tiny suppliers and ten thousand little retailers, each doing whatever it does. There is, of course, "the Japanese people," but that is not an "it" but a "they." Anything you find to say about "the Japanese people" applies only to some of them. They are honest? No, there are gangsters and endless money-politics scandals. Hardworking? I met some construction-industry executives who said they prize Brazilian guest-workers (usually of Japanese descent) because they work so much harder and more willingly than the natives. Homogeneous? Hardly. Generalizations crumble and one is left standing on water.

9

The confusion begins on arrival. Here along the expressway from the airport are landscaped shrubs, carefully trimmed; but they are trimmed not in round bloblike shapes but so that pointy masses stick out irregularly. (Why trim a bush to look like a billiard ball or a sugar cube? It isn't natural.) Here at the downtown terminal is a taxicab with driver and meter, just like home; but he wears white gloves and he will not cheat you. Here is the taxi radio pouring out senseless Asian babble; yet something about the sound nags, until it dawns on you that this is *baseball*. The confusion is a cliché; any American, any foreigner, who has lived or worked here will tell you how the cycle goes. Step one, arrival. Step two, This place is so different! Step three, This place is really just like home! Step four, formation of conclusion: "Now I think

I understand this place." Step five, collapse of conclusion; too many exceptions. Step six, repeat from step two.

10

Asia remains for us Americans a romantic and vaguely frightening place. What we know of it, we know as the alien jungle where Viet Cong and Americans blew each other's brains out, or as Conrad's fragrant land of glamour and death. "There was not a light, not a stir, not a sound," writes Conrad. "The mysterious East faced me, perfumed like a flower, silent like death, dark like a grave." In our hearts we still half expect rickshaws and bowl-shaped haircuts, even in Japan, although we may say and believe that by now we know better. I believed I knew better when I arrived, but I found I was surprised by my ignorance. Japan is not the Asia of Western novels. To find that mysterious Asia now, one has to set out to look for it or invent it, which is just what many foreigners here do. Japan is rather the land of fifty-dollar haircuts on every young man in Tokyo under thirty-five, the land of crisp Eurocut suits, the land of temples and shrines now approximately as hushed and holy as the Bronx Zoo. I am embarrassed to have been surprised by this, but I was. I had heard about the centuries-old xenophobia of the Japanese, and about the pointing and gawking that went on whenever a foreigner appeared outside the biggest cities. I had heard that mothers would point you out to their children as they might a giraffe: Yonder white-colored, big-nosed thing is something you must know about, a *gaijin*, a foreigner. Everyone who came thirty years ago had this kind of experience, and remnants do persist. Sometimes blonde women have their hair stroked on the subway. A boy in Sapporo slyly stroked the hair on my legs (though I am barely any more hairy than the average Japanese); in another place two boys rode by me on a bicycle, and as they passed the older remarked succinctly to the younger: "Gaijin." A strapping, all-American college man I met was approached in Nagoya by a schoolgirl who spoke incomprehensibly to him and then began tugging at the hair on his forearms. Soon he was surrounded by girls, a regular petting zoo, and he didn't know whether to be amused or offended. Yet these are remnants only, and today even the young children, although delighted by a foreigner (new toy), are never shocked or amazed. They know us from our television and from the hordes of us who have descended recently on their country. In Morioka, a town toward the north, I was walking to a museum, which so far had failed to materialize. Across the highway I saw a few small boys and I called out to them in my tourist Japanese, asking how many minutes to the museum. *Go-fun*, five minutes, they called back. I thanked them, congratulating myself on knowing a little of the language. They shouted back, in English, "Five minutes!" In a tiny mountain town of Kyushu, the southern island, I visited a third-grade class. I asked the twenty or so children—they were the entire third grade in this little country school—how many had traveled outside of Kyushu, and only a few raised their hands. I asked how many had met a foreigner, and all but a few hands went up. Mostly they had met Americans. The children wanted to know why my nose was so long, but they were not surprised to see such a nose in their classroom. It was I who was surprised: surprised by their ordinariness. I was to be surprised this way many times. Also disappointed, insofar as one hopes to find here the Real Asia, which is to say the Asia of Western myth.

11

If Japan has an aura of mystery that sets it apart from all the other rich industrial countries, that is in no small measure because the Japanese language does not use the Roman alphabet, or anything like it. This is extremely disconcerting, no matter how fully you try to prepare yourself for it. At first I was incapable even of understanding menus and deciphering fare charts in the train stations. One cannot help but feel the society to be in some elemental way "closed" or unfathomable. I do not believe that I was ever controlled or "handled" by the Japanese, but the shock of dependence is profound and sometimes it was hard not to *feel* handled. Pick up a German or Italian newspaper and you can guess at words and make out sentence structure. Even with Russian you can guess a little. Pick up the Japanese paper, and you can't even tell where words begin and end. You do see Roman spellings on highway signs and subway markers and the like, mainly for the benefit of foreigners. English is also used senselessly as a kind of decoration. The Japanese adorn T-shirts and shop signs with found English, picked up who knows where and applied almost randomly. (Spotted in Yoyogi, a travel agency named thus: "Travel LIV—Luminary of Immensely Voyage." Inevitably—here it is impossible not to be condescending— the slaphappy use of decorative English brings to mind the naïve tribesman who decks himself out with a fan belt for a necklace and a hubcap for a hat.) Decorations aside, however, the business and conversation of the country are notated in code: two separate phonetic syllabaries and thousands of Chinese-style ideograms. Reading and writing are diabolically difficult. Spoken Japanese is another matter; contrary to general belief, it is challenging but not at all forbidding. Still, I understood almost nothing except what came to me through English speakers or what was directed to me in simple, patient Japanese. Fortunately, most members of the intelligentsia and the officialdom speak English. Unfortunately, many of the ordinary people whom you most want to talk to don't speak English. Attempts to fake a snooze on the train while listening intently to a nearby conversation are foiled utterly. On the subway I would strain to overhear a group of girls on their way home from school, but everything was opaque. The ads over their heads, the books in their hands, the newspapers—meaningless. Everywhere I saw surfaces, but nothing beneath. Inevitably, then, the first reaction is aesthetic.

12

The Tokyo in which one finds oneself on the first night is clean, except for cigarette butts. It is not beautiful. In stores and on signs the color sense is superb: rich primary colors well matched. The streets are crowded with black sedans, which are status symbols and so are new and spotless. Hair is moussed. Middle-aged men are not quite so prone to overflow around the middle. One notes on the street a sense of poise and self-confidence, especially among the younger men and women, who dress with great style and care. One would sense instinctively, even knowing nothing else, that this is a society in its building phase. There is a sense, among these men and women, of a people who have hit their stride and know it. Admiration is commanded. Awe, even. This was all rubble forty-five years ago. Before I came here, all the countries I visited lacked America's sharp edge of vitality and open-ended rambunctiousness. Rome, Paris, London—great cities, interesting cities, but somehow they seemed half a step behind. One felt that the news was being received in those cities rather than made. Japan is not rambunctious, but it lacks nothing of vitality. Tokyo throbs with a feeling that what is happening is happening here. The only city that compares to it that way is New York; but New York has a stench of decay and fear.

13

Here is a pachinko parlor, beckoning under blazing neon. To go in is to be flooded by bright light and musical beat and mirrored walls and humming chrome pachinko machines— row upon row of machines, most of them being worked by methodical Japanese, playing game after game. What goes on here? Pachinko is a kind of vertical pinball, but it makes no sense to anyone I know who has tried it. Returning from the rear of the arcade, another American traveler, also new to Japan, reports that the toilet is a ceramic hole in the ground. Apparently one kneels over it—but facing which way? And what does one do with one's pants? Egad! We resolve not to get caught too far from our hotel.

14

You feel perfectly safe among them, and also completely on the outside. As you walk in Roppongi, a busy nightlife district, the closest thing to human contact is a boy's "hi," followed by an excited smile when his magic word elicits the same in return. You notice something different and realize it's that people are quite unfazed by being looked at. Within reason, you can look them straight in the face as you pass on the street. This is provocative if tried in the United States, where eye contact makes women embarrassed or fearful and men hostile or suspicious. But the Japanese either don't notice or don't care. This unaccustomed freedom to gaze raises mixed feelings. On the one hand, it is testimony to Japan's safeness. Someone who looks at you is probably not going to hurt you. In Japan you are about an eighth as likely to be murdered as in America, a thirtieth as likely to be raped. A black male in the United States is forty times likelier to be killed than the average Japanese. On the other hand, one feels slighted, conspicuous yet ignored. I was always a little startled when I was addressed from time to time—for instance, if a bus driver wanted my attention—as *gaijin-san*, "Mr. Foreigner." I suppose I felt the way a black man might feel if he were addressed as "Mr. Black Man." *Gaijin* is very frank. Literally it means "outside person," and nothing could be more apt. It is a close relative of an equally frank and still more important word, *gaikoku*, "foreign country." Our own word "foreign" derives from the Latin for "outside," but over the centuries the connection has been covered. Only a scholar can see it. In Japanese, the connection is impossible to miss, even for a child, since *gaikoku* is nothing but *gai* plus *koku*, "outside" plus "nation." Outnation, outland. Thus the more polite expression for "foreigner," *gaikoku-jin*, literally means "outlander." And that is just how one often feels among them, especially at first: outlandish. On the street in front of the Labor Ministry I was hurrying forward and brushed past a man whose cigarette scraped my sleeve and left ashes. Instantly he said, "Excuse me," in English. He could barely have had a chance to look at me, yet he registered that I spoke English.

15

The people aren't clones. This is immediately evident even if you are unused to looking at Asians and still haven't noticed that the hair comes in infinite fine gradations of blackness: black-black, brown-black, dark brown, even reddish brown. Height varies enormously. I had hoped to come to Japan and feel tall, a luxury denied me since childhood. My wish was fulfilled only when I was among the older generation. The young men averaged somewhere around my height (about five feet seven), and when I visited the high schools I felt positively short.

16

It must be reported that the Japanese are exceptionally beautiful. Though generalizing is hazardous, there is a certain type of beauty that is recognizably Japanese: balanced, self-contained, demurely radiant. At their best the women are lithe and focused and have warm dark eyes, which are shy at first but soon sparkle. There is nothing hard or cynical about the women, but neither are they "seductive" in the American sense, since Japanese men tend to like their women "cute" and this is off-putting to Americans in these postfeminist years. The young men make no attempts whatever to hide their vanity. At their best they have compact frames, with broad shoulders riding above slender waists, and perfect straight carriage and a certain swaggerless lightness of bearing. The skin reminds you that, after all, the Japanese are Pacific islanders, like the Balinese or Polynesians: it is very smooth in texture, glowing gold-brown in color, and set off ideally by the thick black hair. One feels that no other combination—skin brown-gold-pink and hair crisp black—could be as right.

17

Everywhere people were helpful: so much so that I often felt overobliged and thus irritated. One day at the bank I checked my umbrella at the stand by the door and then, half an hour later, forgot that I had left it there. Outside it was raining and so I asked at the desk if anyone had found an umbrella. (There is no inch-thick Plexiglas in Japanese banks to shield the tellers.) No, said the woman, and then ran to fetch me a plastic one, which she begged me to take. Just as she returned with it I realized that my own umbrella was in the rack, right where it belonged. Sheepishly I covered by leaving, "finding" my umbrella, and returning the bank's. Another time I got lost in the human anthill of Shinjuku Station, and asked directions. A man standing with a group of his friends gave instructions, but in fast Japanese. I waded deep into the crowds for five minutes and was lost again. A voice from behind me offered help. The man had left his friends to follow me discreetly, and he did not leave me until he saw that I had found the way.

18

It is no coincidence, this sensitivity. Japanese social systems have softened vastly, almost unrecognizably in some cases, since before the war, but they still are rigorous and sometimes cruel in their demands for diligence, patience, and self-abnegation. Everyone expects everyone to put up with a great deal. What softens the social system's rigor, making it bearable and often cozy, is the high degree of discreet sensitivity shown by people within the system, rounding the edges and easing the weight. We foreigners live divinely in Japan: the social system makes no demands on us, but we enjoy the personal sensitivity. An American I know, who has lived in Japan for many years, concluded at last that the country is a very good and a very bad place. Just when he feels he can put up with no more, something wonderful happens. He loses his wallet somewhere (more than once), and the next day it is on his desk. He does not have to look to see if anything is missing.

19

Knowing of the country's long spell of self-imposed isolation from all foreign contact, one is utterly unprepared for the openness of the people. For more than two hundred years, until the middle of the nineteenth century, the Japanese government forbade its subjects to leave the country or, having left, to return. (The penalty was death.) By restricting travel, sequestering the country's few foreigners, and all but abolishing foreign trade, the rulers insulated themselves from what they deemed to be the destabilizing influence of foreigners. When ports were finally opened under foreign pressure, a wave of revulsion led to widespread unrest under the slogan "Expel the Barbarians!" The Japanese worked hard for many years to build their reputation for xenophobia. Thus today one expects remoteness, indirection, suspicion masked by extravagant politeness; one expects hospitality, yes, but also to be held at arm's length. In fact, one finds rather the opposite, precisely because one is foreign. It is hopeless to come here as an outsider and try to work the system, or, if not hopeless, then frustrating and grueling: all the knobs and levers and buttons are on the inside. To enter any Japanese social system you must first get past the sign on the front door, which invariably says, "By introduction only." I cannot think of Japan without thinking of Kochan, the master sushi chef. He would serve only people who he knew would approach the raw fish in a spirit of humility and seriousness. To screen out the frivolous he required an introduction, and he hid all his fish under the counter. When strangers wandered unintroduced into his tiny Ginza restaurant, he would tell them he was fresh out of everything. I saw this happen once. A couple came in asking for a table. Kochan shook his head: Sorry, no fish today. They knew he was lying, since the restaurant was full of people eating fish—but it was a polite lie, understood for what it was and therefore acceptable. If you try to work the Japanese system without being properly introduced, the polite lie is what you'll get, or maybe just a stony silence. However, if you are content to learn, to explore, to talk, rather than to compete or to join or to operate, then the Japanese lay themselves open to you often with a frankness that takes you aback. They are less voluble than (say) the Italians and less plainspokenly blunt than the Americans, but if you can read between the lines, they show you everything. Foreigners are, indeed, at a peculiar advantage in that respect. We are not part of the circle of evaluators and expecters, we are outside the ring of gossipers and colleagues and relatives, and so we may have confessions blurted out to us, sometimes embarrassingly. The blurted confession is a fine art in Japan, and one much to be savored by the foreign voyeur. An American economist I know was speaking in his office one day on professional matters with a Japanese economist; it was their first meeting. Toward the end of the hour, the Japanese visitor abruptly changed the subject by announcing that he was miserable in his work; what should he do? My astonished friend could only sputter that he really didn't know. "It all comes out, all the unhappiness, all the grievances," Donald Richie writes. "The foreigner is chosen precisely because telling him makes no difference." True, yet I was struck still more by the unspectacular but easy flow of casually intimate information. I asked people's salaries. (Perhaps salaries are a big secret only in America, where money is measure of worth.) I asked people what their life's dream was. No unrecognizable answers were forthcoming. An architect with an entrepreneurial spirit said he wanted a big house, a big boat, and five horses. A journalist said he wanted a log house in the mountains. Various people said they wanted to travel. These are American dreams, perhaps human dreams. They are shabby and mundane, and so true. I asked people whether their lives were satisfying, and here too got truth. An innkeeper in the mountains told me that his dream was to travel, but like many Japanese he took only a few days' vacation every year, and those were enough to take him and the family only as far as nearby Fukuoka. Work was all he had known. Anything else would have to come later, much later, maybe never. I asked him how he would feel about the life he had led if he learned it was soon to end. "*Kanashii*," he said—sad. We Japanese have satisfied our stomachs and our pockets, he said, but not our hearts.

20

I found I could ask anything. I asked a woman of twenty-

five about her marriage plans. Her name was Sumiko and
she said, not meaning to be serious, that she had given up.
The cruel saying here has it that a woman over twenty-five
is a "Christmas cake"—a leftover, stale after the twenty-fifth.
I met Sumiko at an office where I often had business. She
was eager and graceful though not beautiful, and one sensed
in her eyes a power of will as well as the proper Japanese
delicacy. Her job bored her, and so she quit to go traveling,
but not before asking me whether I would like to meet with
her to work on my Japanese. The younger Japanese women
seem especially eager for contact with foreigners. Many of
them, like so many Daisy Millers, go to America or Europe
in their mid-twenties before settling down to the inevitable
drudgery of marriage and children. We walked one night
through the Tokyo bustle and Sumiko told me how much
her parents worried about her failure to marry. Apparently
her father was a man of means but had no sons. Her sister had
married a first-born, an heir in his own right and therefore
unwilling to assume his wife's family name and fortune.
Thus the pressure was on Sumiko to marry a second or third-
born, who could become her father's heir. Failing that, her
father might feel he had no choice but to adopt a male heir. It
all sounded like something out of Chaucer. So, I asked, what
will you do? She intended to marry for love. Eventually, no
doubt, she would find someone. She would have to. Marriage
meant escape from her parents' house, and it meant attaining

an adulthood that would not be seen as weird. Most young men and women simply do not consider the possibility of not getting married; the whole force of the society, bosses and friends and above all family, ensure that this is so. One acquaintance of mine, a Japanese academic in his early thirties, regularly gets called into his dean's office and, by way of a helpful hint, is handed the resume of an attractive female job applicant. An up-to-date intellectual I met spoke with disapproval of the old and (to him) embarrassing custom of *omiai*, the date arranged through relatives or bosses. And (I asked him) what if your own son were not married by thirty or thirty-five? Then, replied the father, I'd ask him to try that embarrassing old custom.

21

In the course of weeks or months the feeling of being on the surface here may diminish. The extent to which it does may depend on your attitude. Some foreigners thrive. I know an American who moved to Japan from Texas and now is master of the *shakuhachi*, a difficult traditional wind instrument, which he teaches to the Japanese. I doubt he will ever live in the United States again. Others always feel like outsiders but are happy not to be Japanese and feel that being an outsider is just as well. Still others grow bitter. They feel they are pushed back, rejected, overridden. Experiences vary widely. My sense is that pushy people and tall people do less well in

Japan. Often, I suspect, Americans have more than their share of problems because so many are know-it-alls. This becomes more evident when the eye and ear grow accustomed to the Japanese sea of black hair and the often annoying Japanese habit of indirection. Endearingly but also tiresomely, we tend to believe that the whole world is American at heart. Scratch the surface of the Hindu cleric or the African tribesman or the Japanese salaryman and you find an American waiting to be liberated—so we often assume, even if we do not always say so. And we are not necessarily wrong. An American man I know went to visit a family in rural Wales, where he was chagrined to discover that he was the only person at the dinner table who was not an avid follower of "Dynasty." Give people the chance to have McDonald's, blue jeans, and democracy, and invariably most of them will seize it. From my room in Japan I could walk in ten minutes to McDonald's (twice), Arby's, Kentucky Fried Chicken, Wendy's, and others. Perhaps, then, it is understandable that Americans go to Japan and play doctor. "Here's what's wrong with your country," we say. "Take two antimonopoly laws and call me in the morning." We all do it, me included (just watch). Also understandably, the Japanese get jaded. They sit quietly, listen respectfully, and think, "Why don't these guys ever shut up?" Once after a binational conference where the Americans had done most of the talking, and indeed had often answered questions posed to the Japanese, I observed to a Japanese participant that Americans were loudmouths. "This," he said dryly, "is a well-known fact."

22

In my own case, the glass wall broke one night in April a few weeks after I arrived. Wholly of its own accord, the neon surface of Tokyo cracked open and Japan never again seemed impenetrable. In central Tokyo, near the prime minister's residence, I was looking for dinner. I stumbled into a yakitori restaurant, a place full of Japanese men and cigarette smoke, and when I said I was alone the hostess put me at the counter. The man on the stool to my right smiled unsurely at me, as though he wanted to say something. He was young and had an open face with a beaming smile and bright eyes, though I recall his eyes were red that night from the day's work. I said or tried to say that I couldn't read the menu. He nodded. At that moment his companion, whose seat I had just taken, returned. I tried to give back the seat but the newcomer gestured emphatically no and sat down on my left. The men I was now sandwiched between turned out to be Messrs. Nakahara and Sasaki. They were both salarymen, low-level white-collar workers at a small trading company nearby. The older bought and sold machine tools, the younger would do the same in five or ten years. Sasaki, the young smiler, was twenty-six, an inch taller than I, and stylishly dressed in an unvented suit with wide shoulders and full-cut pants. He had the vanity of his generation. His hair was done up a little bouffant and he carried a smart leather handbag of the sort that fashionable Japanese men were substituting for wallets. Nakahara was thirty-eight, short, and dressed in the merely serviceable kind of suit that men of his generation typically wore. Goodwill having been established, the problem was to communicate.

23

This proved possible, though it required some ingenuity. That I spoke barely any Japanese, and that they had only a miscellany of English words and phrases ("I haven't seen you lately." "Just a moment please." "OK OK OK!"), made communication difficult. On the other hand, it also made communication possible. Had I met a couple of machine-tool salesmen at a coffee-shop counter in America, we would have had nothing to say to each other; we would have exchanged pleasantries and turned away. These two Japanese men and I were not handicapped by any comprehension of accents or class attachments. That we had nothing to say was not a problem, because anything we managed to say was more than good enough. In the event, we managed to say quite a bit. It was not, granted, the sort of conversation to which Johnson treated Boswell:

I: Where does Nakahara-san live?

Nakahara: In an apartment. Forty-five minutes away, by

train. Very small, fourteen *tatamis*, plus bath. [This would probably be under 300 square feet.] With wife. Small but close to work.

I: Very small, yes?

Nakahara: Yes. When children come, we move. Expensive to live in Japan. Jona-san has a big American house?

I: No. Small apartment. Bigger than Nakahara-san's but still small. Both countries, young people, same problem, expensive house. And Sasaki-san lives where?

Sasaki: In Tokyo, just across the river. [This is in the central city, some of the world's most expensive real estate.]

I: Oh, nice. Very expensive to rent, yes?

Sasaki: No, it is my family's house.

I: A *house*?? In *Tokyo*? Sasaki-san is a rich man!

[Consternation, vigorous shaking of heads. No, no, no, not rich. I am given to understand that this is, in Nakahara's English, "old-time home." I try to get across that if Mr. Sasaki sold his house he and his family could live like princes on the proceeds. But either I am naive or they are—somebody is, anyway. The house has been in the family for years and they wouldn't dream of selling it. It's crowded with people and far from luxurious. It has mice in the ceiling. Thus they are not wealthy. In Japan, wealth is what you produce, not what you own. The subject changes. I am trying to explain where I am from.]

I: Phoenix. In Arizona state. Do you know Phoenix?

[Puzzled looks. I write "Phoenix" on a napkin. Looks like Fonix, doesn't help. Map-drawing ensues. Japan here, California here, Los Angeles here, this is Arizona state, here is Phoenix. Continued puzzled looks, followed by an outburst from Sasaki.]

Sasaki, triumphantly: Yuma Yuma Yuma!

[He has seized the napkin and is pointing, with dead accuracy, to Yuma, Arizona. It turns out that one of the Tokyo baseball teams has a training camp in Yuma. So now we are talking sports. Nakahara professes to be a fan of Konishiki, the American sumo wrestler.]

I: Why Konishiki?

Nakahara, in English: "Training, training."

[This turns out to mean he likes him because he trains hard in the Japanese way. A classic Japanese attitude: high marks for those who try hard in the accepted fashion. Now we are talking about beer. I instruct them eloquently in the pleasures of foreign beer.]

I: This beer, Japanese beer, is OK. But not so good. Bass Ale: much better.

[Oh.]

And so the conversation went. It was scintillating, although you had to be there. After a couple of hours Nakahara wrote a time and date on his business card. In two weeks, same place at 6:30, we would meet again. I went off into the night whistling and exuberant. I liked these two, the genial Nakahara and bright-eyed Sasaki. Two weeks later, when I came back, the restaurant was closed and my salarymen didn't show up.

24

I did, at their office, a few days later. The place was entirely uncarpeted—all shiny linoleum. The furniture was metal. The only women in sight were office ladies (girls, practically, in their premarriage years) dressed in gray and white outfits. Stewardesses, so to speak. The men sat at desks alongside one another, without dividers or any other concessions to privacy. Add sleeve garters and eyeshades, and you were in an American office from the twenties or thirties. At least by American standards, Japanese singularly lack vanity about their offices, except at the very highest levels, where part of the job is to impress visitors. It was not uncommon to find executives sharing offices with their assistants, or even two assistants. And it was quite common indeed for the boss to be set off from his charges only by a desk placed a little farther from the others, or next to the window. If the Japanese are good at working together, it must be partly because they sit together. The Japanese office geography, with its rows of desks placed side by side, implies that everybody knows everything about everybody almost instantly. Foreigners who expect private offices can make mistakes: fail to recognize, for instance, that the man with the corner desk is in fact a powerful official. I went to meet with a division director at the imposing Ministry of International Trade and Industry. Predictably the office turned out to be a buzzing room full of bustling young men in white shirts and of desks arranged side by side in rows. At a table pretty nearly in the middle of everything—this was, so to speak, the conference room— two businessmen sat deep in conversation with a pair of junior officials. They were consulting on business plans and exchanging information. As for the division director, his "office" turned out to be a corner desk with a sofa nearby. We talked and sipped tea while the buzzing went on all around us. Clearly the man knew what was going on in his office.

25

The salarymen had found the restaurant closed and assumed that I wouldn't meet them. My appearance in their office, they later assured me, occasioned no little surprise among their co-workers. We went out for dinner again and then again. Communication became steadily easier. We had a birthday dinner for Mr. Sasaki. We discussed the perils of traditional Japanese toilets, the travails of hair loss, vacations. (They were entitled to extended vacations but never used them; if they were gone for more than a long weekend, bosses would growl, colleagues would be overburdened. Mr. Nakahara had not had a whole week's vacation since his honeymoon. "I don't get no satisfaction," he said, in Rolling

Stones English.) We inspected Mr. Sasaki's life plan. He intended to get married by thirty, for love. If by thirty no love marriage, then an arranged date. If by thirty-five still no marriage, then desperation. Mr. Nakahara had married only a few years ago. One night he announced that his wife was coming to meet us for dinner. He put his fingers in his nose and mouth to make a ghoulish face and declared that she was *oni*. *Oni*? Dictionary check: "ogre, demon, devil." (She turned out to be young, pretty, and shyly amused by her husband's odd friendship.) Thus did we spend evenings in Tokyo, this improbable pair of honest salarymen and I.

26

After a while, a long while, I began to leave my hotel without a map. If you knew your subway stop, somehow you could always find your way home. And the subway would never disappoint, as long as you were aboard before midnight closing time. To my consternation, the subway trains arrived right on schedule, to the minute, even during rush hour when the trains came three or four minutes apart. If the schedule said the trains would come at 5:03, 5:07, and 5:10, they would not come at 5:04, 5:08, and 5:09. At first this struck me as quite the most remarkable and stupid civic accomplishment in the world. But gradually I began to take it for granted. Why shouldn't subway trains come on time? Tokyo is reassuring that way. Of all the world's great cities, it must be the most predictable. New York City may have its nervous electricity, Paris its charm and Rome its warmth, but Tokyo is the one for reliability. I soon had my favorite shops and restaurants. A little basement restaurant in one of the big office buildings adopted me. The hostess knew what I liked and beamed at me when I came in. Every day the food was good.

27

By day Tokyo is best seen from a high place: from one of the high-rise hotels downtown, perhaps. You can look out and on a very clear day see Mount Fuji in the far distance, a quite forgettable sight. More impressive is that the city is vast, enormous; it goes on without letting up for as far as the eye can see. Except for a few recent skyscrapers, the buildings are low. They tend to be squat and gray and nondescriptly new. Excepting perhaps Los Angeles, Tokyo is the only major city I have ever visited that made no architectural impression of any kind. The arterial streets are busy and dull and numbingly interchangeable. On them one could easily lose track of what continent one is on, except for the signs in Japanese. The back streets and alleys, however, are quite Asian, complete with men on bicycles and sometimes cemeteries and shrines. In the back streets one remembers where one is.

28

What saves Tokyo is that even now it is a patchwork of

towns, of neighborhoods. Therefore the city never swamps you; it refuses to overwhelm. It rarely reaches for anything beyond human scale. It is cluttered with ghastly elevated freeways, but mercifully our American-style canyons of black glass and our concrete plazas of desolation, all designed by geniuses to be loved from miles away, are nowhere to be found. Instead one goes, in Tokyo, from one "town" to the next. Toward the center of each town, near the rail station (a subway or commuter line), will reliably be a street lined with little stores, one after another, everything you need, each in its shop. Liquor, sundries, stationery, toys, electronic gizmos, cakes, fruit, yakitori, sushi, coffee, a drink of sake or beer. From the station the streets spread outward and you enter a maze. You are constantly arriving at another corner, turning it, and turning again. The first time you go to someone's house, maybe the second time also, your host will have to send you a map beforehand, showing how to thread the maze. In many American cities, the end of every block is ten minutes away and there is nothing on street level except yawning entrances to underground parking garages. Each endless block is a ghetto. In Japan the short blocks and the parade of little shops and houses create the sense of intimacy without which the Japanese would die of privacy. Often you come upon neighborhoods in which the streets are so narrow that cars must negotiate them with care; the result is a glorious quiet, a Venetian calm.

29

Despite their commercial success and the statistics showing Japan's standard of living near the world's highest, the Japanese will often insist that their country is not rich. And, indeed, outside the glittery sections of Tokyo you would never guess that the nation is wealthy. An American eye gauges wealth by looking at houses, and in Japan those are generally not impressive. The Tudors and Colonials, the rolling lawns, the swimming pools that connote wealth in America are not to be found in Japan. Middle-class housing tends to be boxy and serviceable. Newer developments have that combination of comfortableness and vacuousness which in America became known as ticky-tacky. However, you almost never see dinginess; like violence and spontaneity, dinginess is rarely committed. And one feature of the houses is quite remarkable, so much so as to dominate all impressions. This is the roof. It is sloped, gently curved as though someone above were lifting the corners ever so slightly, and covered with convex clay tiles, usually dark gray, sometimes other colors. Its corners and edges are carefully finished. Viewed from above, the gray roofs of temples and houses make towns look like dense colonies of armored sea creatures. I am told that these tile roofs are expensive—they certainly look it—and that they last as long as a hundred years. (What does it say about a people that they would invest in a hundred-year roof?) By comparison, asphalt shingling is mere paper. An elaborate roof may be multitiered, rising several levels: roofs over roofs. But even the less expensive houses typically aspire to partial tiling, at least. A house is naked otherwise. It is built, so to speak, from the top down. "The significance of the roof in Japanese architecture is confirmed by the word for roof itself," writes Heino Engel. "For the two Chinese ideograms, *ya-ne*, for the Japanese word for roof mean nothing but 'house' (interior) and 'root' (source). Roof is the very root of the house." In a communitarian society, perhaps, once shelter is provided for, walls are less important.

30

By night Tokyo sheds its blandness and unfolds. After dark it is best seen not by looking down from a skyscraper but by burrowing deep into the underbrush of bars and restaurants, where the Japanese go to heal themselves and to complain after the day's brutalities. In Shinjuku the bars are stacked six and seven high. You can press all the buttons in the elevator and see a different bar every time the door opens—a train bar ("The Amtrak"), an oldies bar, a cowboy bar, a disco bar, a bar bar. As for the little (and big) restaurants, the Ginza and Azabu and Shinjuku and, indeed, the side streets of Japanese cities generally are crammed so full of them that you wonder who ever eats at home. Inside they are snug and beery.

31

Outside, on the big street corners, is Tokyo's legendary neon. In Shinjuku especially, though not only, you gaze up at towers of neon. Where but here can you see "Mr. Donut" in two-story neon, high atop a building? Even tastelessness—especially tastelessness—is done immaculately. Interestingly, there is never a hint of unwholesomeness. The pornographic movie house I visited in Ueno has a downstairs if you want to see men with women, upstairs for men with men. It was dark, of course, and shabby, with a ticket taker who was careful not to look too hard at you. No one lingered on the street in front of it. But sleaze and danger were nowhere to be sensed. Like everything else in Japan, the place was crisp, commercial, tame. By contrast, Times Square positively stinks with shame and fear.

32

In April came flowers to Hibiya Park, in the center of Tokyo. The park was impeccably manicured, with benches around a lawn (grass cut very short) and a central arrangement of tulips and palms. If you had the time, you could sit there eating lunch and furtively studying the homeless men. There aren't many in Tokyo, but you do see them. Wafting past me, from the next bench, came the scent of the man lying asleep. Another who looked just like him shambled past: long black hair, dark tattered clothes, a disconnected expression. One day, deep in the jungle of videotape machines in a high-tech electronics store, I saw a young woman crouching on the floor in the corner, obsessively shouting again and again in a child's Japanese something about a train. Near her stood a couple of store clerks, entirely at a loss. Everyone was embarrassed.

33

I felt, as time went on, that Washington, D.C., receded into the far distance and then reemerged as a mile-high caricature, alternately coaxing and screeching. At National Airport, arriving travelers used to be greeted by banners proclaiming Washington the most important city in the world. In America, sensible people rightly laughed at the District of Columbia's childish puffery. In Tokyo, sensible people would not have seen the joke. Japan today is very largely a product of two defining traumas of conflict with the West, and in both cases "the West" was specifically the United States government. The second trauma was World War II and the subsequent American occupation, which erected lasting democracy and established Japan as America's little brother and junior partner—at least until recently. The first was in the 1850s, when Japan, which was still dwelling under government-enforced seclusion from the rest of the world, was forcibly opened by Commodore Perry and his fleet. The Japanese found themselves helpless before Perry's modern cannon (in

1853 he arrived with four men-of-war, including two under steam), and they reacted with a two-pronged strategy. In the short term, placate; in the longer term, catch up. Ever since, they have been placating (except, of course, in the militarist period) and catching up. To this day, Washington looks from Tokyo like a giant whose every mood must be carefully monitored and reacted to. When some American goofball writes a book or makes a speech about Japan's plot to take over the world, the American papers ignore or bury it, but the Japanese papers put it on page one. "Japan Bashing Reaches New Heights; Crisis in U.S.-Japan Relations!" (I speak from experience: in one such instance the goofball was me. A few banal words which I said off the cuff at a dinner for some visiting Japanese parliamentarians wound up being billed on the front page of the *Mainichi Shimbun*, absurdly, as showing what powerful Americans really think of Japan.) Tokyoites and Washingtonians share, alas, the same mischievous delusion, namely that Washington is the center of the world. A neurotic geography, this. Even though you know better, you find you pick it up.

34

After a while I gathered my courage and began traveling around the country. For the rambling nerd, there is no better country than Japan: it's the exotic East (pagodas! Buddhas!), but all the pay phones work and you're never out of sight of a convenience store. I ventured first to Osaka and Kyoto and then to smaller cities. It's often said that Tokyo is to Japan as New York is to the United States. And this is true, but only up to a point. For one thing, Tokyo is to Japan as New York City, Washington, D.C., and the state of California bundled up together would be to the United States, so centralized has Japan become. For another, New York is a world unto itself. You can grow up there and have no idea what a small town might be like. The smaller cities of Japan, however, will be manageable once you have mastered the "towns" of Tokyo. You will emerge from the train station and everything will be there: the shopping street dense with little stores, the bigger department stores, the roads radiating outward into quiet neighborhoods, till at last the rice fields begin. Beyond them lie the mountains or the sea.

35

A good way to see Japan: visit video-game parlors. Every city is full of them. I made video stops from Okinawa in the far south to Sapporo in the far north. I never was any good at playing the games myself. Mostly I watched the young and youngish Japanese of both sexes who, typically, didn't mind in the least. The best I ever saw was in Tokyo, a beige-suited young salaryman about five feet high who played Tetris on a single coin, unbeatable, until the arcade closed and he had to stop. *Sugoi*, "wow," I told him, as he finally left, and he nodded almost imperceptibly in acknowledgment. Most were not as good, but they all tried hard. That above all is what the Japanese teach their children: virtue means trying your hardest. I saw a lot of what I wish for myself in these young Japanese—modesty, seriousness without solemnity, and gentleness of deportment. In connection with them a phrase enters the mind that has become dusty and quaint in America: they seem well brought up. They can also seem, however, vacuous. The Asian martial tradition teaches them that endurance in the face of pain or defeat is in itself a quality to be admired, never mind whether enduring makes any sense. I visited a vocational school where students are forbidden to use the elevator because the administration believes that walking up and down stairs—seven stories to the top—is good for the health. There is also a certain well-drilled literalness. One Sunday I was out and about with a few university students who, I realized at one point, were talking merrily about how long my nose was. Retaliating good-naturedly, I demanded to know how the Japanese could smell anything with noses so absurdly small. "You see," said a young man, a medical student, "actually nose size has nothing to do with the ability to smell. That has to do with nerves within the nose. Nose size is related to climate; the bigger nose warms the olfactory membranes. So as far as the sense of smell is concerned, we smell as well as you do." I thought about explaining that I had been kidding, but instead just thanked him.

36

The cities are made for walking. In Kyoto, through the inevitable pedestrian shopping mall, then out into a main artery where the fashionable strolled; into the alleys to hunt for a suitable restaurant; and then, after dinner, up and down the nighttime streets of old Gion, through crowds around bars and clubs, over a bridge where a man with a guitar sat singing "Yesterday," down along the river, where students were wading and splashing in knee-deep water, and then past young couples sitting entwined in darkness along the shore. At every stage along the way, restaurants and places to shop. Japan is commercial if nothing else.

37

Much the most beautiful are the smaller towns. Here the streets are even narrower, the sense of quiet and safety even more profound. In Umemachi, population about 4,500, I was taken to one of the local shrines. After tea we stood on the green hillside looking down over the town: tiled roofs and smoking chimneys and little rice fields all nestled together, and beyond them Kyushu's wooded hills set in receding rows, higher and higher into the afternoon haze. In all Japan I never saw a finer sight than of that town lying in repose under the afternoon sun. It might have been a hamlet from an earlier age—though soon enough you learn that the young are fleeing these villages, leaving emptiness behind.

38

In the movement from one town to the next, time dilates, recedes. Minutes are occupied, dwelt in, rather than "used." You get nothing much done, you cease to care, yet things *do* get done. American time neurosis (a minute is "wasted" unless something is "accomplished") unwinds. In the nondescript northern town of Hakodate one evening I went out of my way a couple of blocks to see the ocean. Night was falling and the sky was foggy, so everything was grayish blue. There was no beach; rather a low seawall and below it a jumble of concrete slabs piled to break the surf. The water made sizzling sounds as it washed ashore. A couple of people fishing. Blackness gathering on the horizon. Lights out to sea. Trash and beer cans. Desolate, beautiful. Nothing happened.

39

You mustn't hurry through Japan. Not only will you miss the show, but people will be annoyed with you. To welcome you they will be generous with their time, and if you are always getting up and rushing off, they will wonder what it is that is so much more important. Rarely do people want to dive right into business; they share time together first, so as to establish a commitment. Social time scales, too, are extended. For the foreign visitor, the question of how to leave parties becomes a delicate one. On weekends I would be invited for an afternoon party beginning at two or three, and it would still be going strong at eight. Finally I would make excuses to leave, feeling like a member of the old Supreme Soviet who is barging out before the end of the party leader's five-hour speech. The truth was that I had no pressing business at home. It was just that at such a party I was "getting nothing done." To me, efficiency has always meant moving through tasks as quickly as possible, and then counting them up at the end of the day. I am always leaving jobs three-quarters finished—finished enough—there's so much to do—and hurrying on to the next thing. This is not the Japanese way. The Japanese reminded me of a remark attributed to Gypsy Rose Lee, the striptease artist, who said that anything worth doing is worth doing slowly.

40

In Japan, efficiency has more to do with perfection than with speed. The famous Japanese preoccupation with quality control is, I think, the natural outgrowth of an aesthetic that calls for every detail to be dwelt upon as though essential and every moment to be wholly occupied. The task at hand is everything: all thought of other tasks and other moments is to be banished. The Japanese sense of beauty is sometimes described as "refined," but a much better word is "concentrated." The aesthetic of concentration can be seen on assembly lines and in schools. Its purest expression, however, is in the Noh, which at its best is a startling experience. Noh is an ancient kind of drama, passed down intact from the fourteenth century. Texts are brief (you can read a whole Noh play in ten minutes), stories are simple, music sparse and unmelodic. Plays may lack even action and character. As for the actors, their gestures are stylized, their faces masked or expressionless, their inflections almost non-existent. "The lines," writes Donald Keene, "are delivered in so muffled and stylized a manner as to be almost unintelligible unless one already knows the text by heart, and the actors make little differentiation in expression between saying 'I am suffering unbearable agony' and 'The cherry trees are in blossom.'" Thus stripped of recourse to dialogue, spectacle, rapid movement, and surprise, the dramatic event succeeds or fails entirely insofar as it achieves concentration. Where concentration is lacking, the Noh is excruciatingly dull, not to mention strange. But when concentration is present, the Noh is enthralling, mesmerizing, commanding. To my amazement, I sat riveted one day as an actor did ostensibly nothing but walk with almost inhuman slowness around the periphery of the stage. I say "ostensibly" because in fact the actor was "doing" a great deal. So intently did he control his rhythm and step, so utterly had he mastered even the slightest extraneous finger twitch or lip tremor or eye movement, that one could imagine his procession continuing untouched through a tornado. Between each footfall, a suspension, a lifetime. The pressure that can be built up in this way, through concentration on momentary perfection, is extraordinary. "No one," writes Donald Richie, "has ever made a mistake on the Noh stage; no one has ever forgotten a line; there are no stumbling entrances, no halting exits. No indulgence is permitted and . . . the performance is without error." This cannot be literally true; yet in the Noh theater on a good day, error seems wholly out of the question. It's no wonder, I suppose, that a culture which can bring off so improbable a nondrama can also build a good car. A car happens to be useful. The Noh or the tea ceremony is not particularly useful. But from the point of view of the Japanese aesthetic, they are all beautiful in much the same way. The beauty is not so much in the product as in the concentration achieved in the making of it.

41

I got used to Japan. I liked the safety and the scale. I liked the measured, determined rhythms. There was, however, a singularity: however comfortable I became, there were undertones that unsettled, paradoxes that discomfited. For instance, here were people whose hospitality was beyond cavil, whose gentleness I witnessed every day. Yet one would hear stories like the one I was told by a man who played baseball on his company's team. A young member of the team was an ethnic Korean—that is, his grandparents were born in Korea but his native language and culture were Japanese.

He was in love with a Japanese woman. They wanted to marry, but her parents forbade it, saying they would cut her off completely if she married a "Korean." So determined was he to win the girl that he was devoting himself to baseball; he would become a star in the big leagues and thus finally win the parents' approbation. (Think of the black Americans who won esteem through sports.) The trouble was that the young man didn't have the talent to get to the big leagues. He wasn't going to make it. I thought I had never heard a sadder story. It is not, however, an uncommon sort of tale. I asked a kind and well-educated Japanese man how he would feel if his daughter were to marry a Korean. He supposed he would get used to it—but his wife, that was another matter. Younger people are not necessarily different. I asked some university students whether they might, perhaps, marry an ethnic Korean or other "foreigner." Their answer was no.

42

I have mentioned that if you read about Japan you will emerge with two pictures that don't fit. Well, go to Japan, live in Japan, and there are *still* two pictures (at least), and they *still* don't fit. You are simultaneously lulled and alarmed. Every so often, just when you had managed to become comfortable, the contradiction would erupt in your face. One incident in particular stands out. On one of those sticky rainy-season days in Tokyo that make you wish you could go indoors even when you are indoors, I was looking for my way outside the Mitaka train station. I needed to know which bus to take. Someone directed me to a bus attendant who spoke some English. His job was to blow a whistle, signal pedestrians to wait, and wave a bus through whenever one left the station. A completely unnecessary job. He looked about forty, and had been studying English since he was nineteen, mainly at the YMCA. I was surprised. It is common for international-ized professionals of the intellectual class to speak English; but there are not many English-speakers among the Japanese bus-attendant class. I asked him: Why do you want so much to learn English?

Because, he said, I like freedom and democracy.

Well. I asked him what freedom and democracy had to do with learning English. He explained that in English one speaks to anyone in more or less the same way, and so one can be more direct. Japanese is layered with levels of politeness, so finely graded, and so finely interwoven with the grammar and the society, that few nonnative speakers ever fully master the art of speaking in just the right way to every person. We have a little bit of this in English: "Yes, sir," when we are being very respectful, "Yeah" to our kids. Once a Japanese man I know who used to be high in the government dem-onstrated how he might conduct a dinnertime conversation if the minister were sitting on his right and a junior official on his left: he spoke formally and elaborately to the one side, barked casually and curtly to the other. This becomes second nature. Nowadays the hierarchic distinctions, though fossilized in the language, are less important than they used to be. But one does need to know what is appropriate. A young academic I met who had returned after studying for some years in the United States had trouble with the senior professors until she relearned to bow instinctively to them (more like a nod, really) whenever she passed them in the hall. This, no doubt, is the sort of thing that the bus attendant had in mind when he said he felt freer speaking English. I prodded him: But Japan is a democracy, isn't it, a free country? He replied, on the surface, yes. When I asked what it was below the surface, he said, and I quote: "It's a feudal system based on personal relationships."

I mentioned that many Japanese seemed happy with the system; he indicated that he was not; my bus pulled up and I left, still feeling astonished. What is one to make of it? On the one hand, if Japan were really so feudal and oppressive, this blue-collar sociologist could hardly exist. "The fact that such a man could talk to you that way," said a Japanese government man when I told him the story, "goes to show how well educated and liberal this country is." On the other hand, clearly the bus attendant was not crazy. Actually, quite a few people speak of Japan, which after all was still a feudal country when Abraham Lincoln was president, as the last redoubt of feudalism; this is something of a cliché among intellectuals. But you do not expect to hear such an analysis, stated with such force and evident conviction, from a bus attendant at the train station. Is there anything to it? A great deal, no. Something important, yes. Something embedded in the Japanese sense of justice. To see it, one must look not at Japan's people but at her social institutions.

43

One must always be careful to distinguish between people and social institutions. I liked the Japanese—much more, indeed, than I had planned to. I did not much like their social institutions, although I came to distrust my feelings about them, since success is hard to argue with. The Japanese are quite open and transparent; but their social institutions are quite otherwise. For the foreign explainers, it is the social systems that are elusive and must be grasped. It is they that confuse and confound us. I found that I began to understand them when I grasped the meaning of Japan's national lies.

44

"Lies" in a mild sense, a nonmoral sense. "Lie" not in the sense of an attempt to deceive others, but of a useful self-deception: a social myth, a public belief, that is necessary and convenient, like Christendom's God and heaven. The myth breaks down or becomes a hindrance eventually, because it is not true, but while it lives it is unfailingly revealing. You can hardly learn more about someone than by looking at the lies he tells himself.

45

The first is the myth of homogeneity, recounted from parent to child as folklore and invoked as the explanation for everything, from economic success to a low crime rate to good schools. In its stronger form it is a tribalist lie, insofar as it says that people come in types and that "our" type, the Japanese type, have something in common because of common ancestry. Tribalism says that "we" are the same in some fundamental way because we share the same blood and heritage, and outside tribes and traditions have not mixed in. This virus is in the air in Japan, and often foreigners who stay in the country catch it. One bright young American I met announced to me earnestly that implacable self-discipline is in the Asian blood. Of course, the truth is that common blood is no real commonality at all. In all cases, including the Japanese case, the differences between individuals within presumed kinds are vastly greater than the similarities.

46

Nonetheless, although I thought I knew better, I was startled by the enormous differences I found, because I had read so much about the people's conformity and sameness. Homogeneity of broad physical type—that is, "Asianness"—

was the only kind of homogeneity that I found, and even this broke down into meaninglessness in particular cases. The Japanese are no more alike than you and I are. Again and again I met people, including many who spoke no English, with whom I felt more in common than I do with many Americans I meet. I found no fundamental similarity, no template, no recipe for Japaneseness. The closest thing to such a recipe, perhaps, is the general belief that one exists: the belief that somehow *wareware nihonjin*, "we Japanese," are all alike, and the willingness to act as though this were true.

47

Time and again I talked to Japanese, especially of the intellectual class, who saw themselves as the rare individualist in a crowd of conformists; and after I had lost count of the rare individualists I had met, I began to get suspicious. A student at a meeting of his university's English-speaking society plopped down in the seat next to me to say that the Japanese are groupists, conformists, trees that all bent before the wind—except him, of course. He was an individualist. One day I was giving a speech in northern Japan. The subject turned to Japan's rice market, which is closed to imports and which everyone knows is sacred. I asked how many people favored liberalizing the market— and the great majority of hands went up. I was surprised, but the audience was more so: each had assumed he was the rarity. It was easy for me to see how different from one another the Japanese are, but it was not easy for them. They have taught themselves not to look for what cannot be. This is true in every conformist society, including America's. Ask an American homosexual what it is like to grow up feeling that he is the only one in the world who is different, and that everyone else is the same. Only later does he discover the lie. Japan is, in that sense, a nation of closet cases.

48

Undeniably you do see fewer outward signs of human diversity in Japanese society than in American society, but that is an artifice, a strategy. The myth of homogeneity isn't substantially true in any nontrivial way, but it is behaviorally true, insofar as it shapes expectations and pretense. Why do people work so hard to preserve it? In order to cope with the most basic of all social problems: the problem of conflict.

49

In a world of staggeringly diverse human belief and preference, conflict is a fundamental social fact. It will happen one way or another, and one way or another it must be managed. So far history has produced, speaking very broadly, three general classes of social systems for managing conflict. One, predominant for many centuries, is the authoritarian model, in which a particular person or group is in charge.

Recently it has tended to be superseded by a different model—namely, that of the liberal social system: a set of public rules that establish an open-ended, depersonalized, usually competitive process for resolving conflict. These systems are open-ended in that the rules are set in advance, but never the outcome; and the rules themselves are subject to change through the operation of the system upon itself (we can vote to change the Constitution). Liberal systems are depersonalized in that no one is supposed to get special treatment merely because of who he happens to be. One such process, such "game," is the voting game, to decide who can use force and when: democracy. Another is the property-trading game, to decide who gets how much of any limited resource: market capitalism. The third is the public criticism game, to decide whose belief is right: science. Together the three games define the liberal age. Their collective evolution is, indeed, the most important social advance in the history of the species. Decentralized public games turn human diversity into a resource: the more people and preferences are put into play, the better. Public games provide the means to choose collectively between competing alternatives, and so they make conflict an engine of constructive change. They have proven to be incomparably successful at exploiting our differences while keeping conflict manageably local and society reasonably stable.

50

However, there is another kind of strategy: avoiding conflict or suppressing it. We all use this strategy to one degree or another. We keep our conversations friendly by saying, "I never discuss religion or politics." We join churches or clubs in which everyone can find common ground. We make friendships and draw on their credit to buy agreement and to preempt tension. All of this is healthy and essential. But a system that relies heavily on avoiding conflict is precarious, because the ineradicable reality of human diversity never ceases to apply pressure from every side. Conflict always remains a threat.

51

Japan relies more heavily on conflict-avoidance than any society I have ever seen. It seeks to deny the reality of conflict by emphasizing, at every turn, the fundamental alikeness of "we Japanese" and dismissing differentness as incidental. Conflict-avoidance is the meaning of the proverb *Deru kugi wa utareru*, "The nail that sticks up gets hammered down." And the *deru kugi*, the nonconformist, is it really hammered down? Sometimes yes, sometimes no. Often it is ignored, tolerated, indulged, even loved or enjoyed. It is not, however, viewed as being in principle a thing of value or a resource; it is viewed as a quirk, as perhaps amusing or interesting but in any case not useful. Conflict-avoidance is also the meaning of *shoganai.* Everyone who comes to Japan has a shoganai story, a story of people who shrug and say: "It can't be helped." I first heard "shoganai" from my salaryman friend, Mr. Nakahara. In the yakitori restaurant he told me how he used to spend three hours each day on jammed trains commuting to and from work. He would rise early in the morning and come home after his wife had gone to bed. Every day, the same ordeal. A hard life, I said, baiting him to complain. "Shoganai," he said. I didn't understand, so he wrote it down in capital letters: SHOGANAI. "It can't be helped." Actually, people do help things here, all the time, the same as they do everywhere else. The salaryman, after all, had finally moved closer to town. But they would not expect to help things. In America, if helping things means confronting someone, then so be it—we confront. In Japan, when helping things would engender conflict, then perhaps things "cannot be helped." Better to steer around the confrontation. Kazuko Tsurumi, the sociologist, writes of a woman stricken with mercury poisoning, the famous Minimata disease, and thereby stigmatized. One day when she was walking a man came from behind and pushed her toward a bluff facing the sea; she barely escaped falling. Ten years later, the man came to her house to apologize. And in between, how many policemen had she complained to, how many lawsuits had she filed? "Ten years ago," she told Tsurumi, "I did not say a word, but just endured. If I had said anything against him, that would have been the end of our relationship. Endurance brought him back to sense. That is the meaning of a communal way of living."

52

An American I know, who lives in Tokyo with his Japanese wife, told me a story. One day his wife discovered that their new drycleaner was overbilling them. My friend was furious. He was going straight to the cleaner's to complain. "No, no," his wife said firmly. To confront the cheater directly would only result in heated denials and a messy scene. Nothing good could come of it. "That is not the way to handle this," she said. "Not in Japan." The next morning, when the boy came from the cleaner's, there was no laundry for him. Next day, still no laundry. And the next and the next. And on the following day, the drycleaner himself appeared at their door. "It seems," he said, after abjectly apologizing, "there has been a mistake and you were overcharged. I am refunding your money, and of course you have my personal assurance that this will not happen again." My American friend was impressed. Not only had their money been returned, but they had let the chiseler know he had been found out—with no fuss, no row, no confrontation. Now that the drycleaner had learned his lesson, they could begin the business relationship afresh. "No," his wife replied, just as firmly as before. "He tried to cheat us. We will never use him again. Nothing can change that."

53

In their striving to suppress confrontation, the people are mutually coercive and, more important, self-coercive. They make a common compact to steer away from conflict and to emphasize commonality. But there is no overbearing central authority, nor is the system much prone to the grossest kind of abuses, because gross abuses would lead to conflict, which would bring infamy on anyone who caused it. Abuses do occur, of course. The system has a dark, Prussian side. In 1990 a high-school teacher in Kobe, determined to teach tardy students a lesson, killed a fifteen-year-old girl accidentally when he forced shut the school's heavy iron gate as she and other last-minute arrivals tried to squeeze through. The girl had never been late for school before, the newspaper said. The case caused outrage around the country. Nonetheless, in the summer of 1991 the principal of a tiny rural private school caught two teenagers smoking and locked them for forty-five hours in a windowless storage shed, where they both died of heat prostration. Yet Prussian excess is rarer than one would expect; and the conflict-suppression system looks less oppressive in person than on paper. One of the big surprises that Japan held for me was that I could not bring myself to feel that the conflict-avoidance regime was sinister, although I tried. Partly this is because the self-coercive aspect is coupled with a high degree of personal sensitivity and responsibility. Partly it is because these are good times for Japan, and the system has not turned abusive as it did in the thirties. And partly it is because so much diversity, indeed so much conflict, thrives in Japan while people look the other way and pretend not to see it.

54

An American I met was asked by a Japanese woman whether he did not, in his heart, wish he were Japanese. He replied: Every morning I get up and thank God I'm not Japanese. At a coffee shop in Kyoto (the Tasty Plaza, no less), I met a twenty-one-year-old waiter who told me that he aspired to live in, of all places, Brazil. Brazil? Why Brazil? Because he had heard that there is great personal freedom in Brazil. He spoke hardly any English, but he knew enough to say that Japan is "not liberal." The repression of conflict, even if voluntary, inevitably leads to feelings that one is under restraint. In Japan, the nexus of conflict resolution is the personal, mutual relationship rather than the impersonal, public process. Conflict in Japan is like sex: such business is all right as long as it is taken care of between intimates and behind closed doors. And the Japanese are both the beneficiary of the conflict-settling relationship and its captive. "Japanese," write three Japan scholars, Ellis S. Krauss, Thomas P. Rohlen, and Patricia G. Steinhoff, "rarely feel they have the option to leave a relationship. Without the options of either exit or expression, the lack of cathartic resolution and fundamental adjustment in the relationship may produce a deep and persistent sense of malaise. This outcome implies that it is the individual, rather than the group or society, who bears the cost of conflict in Japan." Shoganai. It can't be helped.

55

But I see that my high-flying theorizing has led me straight into the trap that I set out to avoid. I have made Japan sound like Mars.

56

Everyone falls into this trap, lured by a second national lie—really an international lie, promulgated within the country and perpetuated without: Japan is Different. Not different in the way that Mexico or Morocco is different, but in its values and culture a place apart, a place alien and vaguely lunar, a deep counterpoint to the West, a society standing slightly outside of and at an angle to the rest of the universe, a place where logic loses its traction and the conventional forces of economics do not apply and the social geometry is non-Euclidean, and so forth and so on. There is altogether too much of this.

57

It so happens that there is truth in most of the observations about Japan's differentness from the West (wherever that is), and it also happens that to look for and dwell upon differences is natural and useful. But with Japan matters have tended to get out of hand. This is in no small measure the fault of the Japanese, with their puerile talk of Japanese snow being different and Japanese intestines being longer and Japanese bees being more communitarian and "No one but a Japanese can really understand us," and all the rest. Every foreigner who goes to Japan (I am told that this is true generally in Asia) will, if he can use two chopsticks with one hand, be congratulated often on his amazing dexterity. *O-hashi ga jozu desu, ne!* Look how well you use chopsticks! One day I was eating at a sushi restaurant when a half-drunk, gnomish old man sitting nearby began to rhapsodize loudly and embarrassingly about my special soul, my unique understanding, my rare sense for the fish. Such a wonderful foreigner, to appreciate sushi! I suppose it's hard to blame him for his silliness. His country held itself apart from the world for a very long time; even today one of the clichés is that Japan is "in the world but not of it." In the literature and popular imagination of the Japanese, Japan itself is the outsider to the world. It is the outnation, the *gaikoku*. Just as the Japanese have tended to tell themselves old wives' tales about their sameness, so they have told themselves old wives' tales about their singularity, and I suspect for the same reason: to wish away the reality of conflict and unruly diversity. Westerners eagerly lapped up the myth, for such glamorous hogwash is romantic. One day in the library, browsing among the books on Japan, I began to see a pattern among the titles. *Queer Things about Japan. A Fantasy of Far Japan* (nonfiction). *Unfathomed Japan. Secrets of Japan. Oddities in Modern Japan.* I plucked out *The Enigma of Japanese Power,* by Karel van Wolferen, and noticed that on the back cover was written only this sentence: "Inside Japan, nothing is quite as it seems." Good for literary business, this queer, fantastic, unfathomed, secretive, odd, enigmatic Japan, where nothing is quite as it seems. "Japan," wrote the American essayist Pico Iyer in his lovely book *Video Night in Kathmandu,* "was the world's great Significant Other," "quite the most alien society I had ever visited," "at heart [it] seemed a secret society," "its assumptions were so different from those of the West that to understand it seemed scarcely easier than eating a sirloin steak with chopsticks." We come to Japan looking for a place that is Different with a big D, a different *kind* of place; and so we find it. For we do not want Japan to be ordinary, whatever else it may be. That would be so boring. We still invoke deep cultural hocus-pocus when we talk about Japan in ways that we do not when talking about, say, Brazil, and we still attribute various successes and failures of the Japanese to various inherent Japanese peculiarities, and we remain too quick to conclude that Japan has invented, for example, a whole new kind of economy. Like lazy taxonomists, we invent new categories when perhaps we should be stretching the old ones. I succumb, too.

58

And so, I suppose, I sometimes should, for Japan is different, and that is an unblinkable fact. Yet nowhere could I find enough differentness to convince myself that the place is *especially* different: not in the restaurants or companies or shops or streets, not on the farms or in the factories or in the schools. Mexico is different. Israel is different. Arkansas is different. Japan is different. And that's the whole story. Japan is, alas and thank God, just another ordinary different place, peopled with all the familiar types.

59

I began to suspect that people were going overboard about Japan's strangeness early on, when I made the inevitable Yankee pilgrimage to the baseball stadium to see the Yomiuri Giants play the Yakult Swallows. Baseball is a national passion, and it makes irresistible fodder for crosscultural comparison. Japanese teams are more authoritarian and militaristic in structure; they stress teamwork over grand slams; they train themselves half to death; they emphasize avoiding errors, so that the style of play is precise, predictable, and dull—even duller, I mean, than American baseball. All this is true. But it is still baseball. I had read about the fans' doing everything in creepy collectivist unison, cheering together and singing together and holding up props together in a weird triumph of organization over fun. "Here was passion by remote control," wrote Iyer of his own Giants game pilgrimage. "And every time I saw ten thousand fans filling the air in unison with black-and-yellow bullhorns, I found myself shuddering a little at the militarism of the display—and at its beauty." No: he has missed the point, missed it subtly but by a mile. The younger fans massed in the cheap seats (half the stadium for each team's fans) *do* hold up umbrellas, for example, in organized waves, chant under the direction of cheerleaders with whistles, and sing songs and pound bangers en masse. There are four teams in the stadium: two on the field and the other two in the outfield stands. Yet a triumph of organization over fun it assuredly is not. The enjoyment was so evident that I longed to join in. And the scene had a haunting familiarity, which at last resolved itself into a memory: in the seventies we kids used to go again and again to see *The Rocky Horror Picture Show*, and we brought our bag of tricks and rituals. On cue, everyone would flick cigarette lighters, throw rice, sway and sing together. The baseball fans were having just the same kind of party, but doing it bigger and going all the way.

60

Often in Japan I had this feeling: of the familiar reaching out to me from the center of the strange—of the foreign crowd filled with faces I thought I recognized. In a small town I stayed for a night with a young man who had never left

Japan, a Shinto priest like his ancestors for many generations before him. Yet we talked like college chums till two in the morning. I felt somehow that I knew him. And over time the social systems also began to look familiar. We know them, I believe, from other places and times, none of them the least bit exotic. The mix is different, the details are characteristic, but the broad outlines are nothing we have not seen before.

61

The economic system looks a lot like that of America a hundred years ago, in the days of the company towns and the great producer trusts and cartels, when big business hid behind high tariff walls and Americans were busy grabbing and improving foreign technology, before the populists demanded their share and the Progressives busted the trusts. Socially Japan looks a lot like America in the 1950s. Everyone notices this, and it's true. In the city of Oita, it struck me again and again, with almost spooky force: the white-bread conformity, the intense devotion without a trace of self-consciousness to business and matters economic (the business of Japan is business), the breadwinner-and-housewife family, the milk bottles and white shirts, the undershirts worn even in ninety-degree weather, the family bowling nights, the gas stations where two attendants run out (I mean *run* out) to meet each arriving car. The adolescent innocence, too. Granted, in this respect, as in some others, Japan looks more like America in the fifties than America ever did. One day a professor at Tokyo University told me that an upperclassman he knew had come to school beaming with satisfaction. The young man, it turned out, had succeeded in holding hands with a girl. (In many ways, teenagers are like children in Japan.) And the political system, with its longtime one-party domination and its close intertwining of ruling party, bureaucracy, and powerful private interests all doing favors for each other—what about that? Mayor Daley would not have failed to recognize it. It is, indeed, nothing stranger than a nationwide case of Chicago in the 1950s.

62

Yes, yes. But what about the Japanese values, whose peculiarity has been so often noted? *Of course* the institutions look familiar: they were imported from the West. Capitalism, in its modern internationalist corporate dress, came with the Meiji Restoration a century ago, when Perry's guns forced the Japanese leadership to see that they must modernize or die; so did science. Democracy, after a stifled infancy, came with the American occupation after the war. But the former two were adopted for expediency, as the best means by which to catch up with the West and so escape its domination; the latter came at the point of a gun. Liberal social systems were grafted—always from above—onto the traditional Japanese values. The Japanese handled the resulting conflicts, characteristically and pretty effectively, by not deigning to notice that they existed. Over time, as people got used to going through the motions of liberalism, and as attitudes followed practices (they always do), Japanese society was liberalized. Teach an old dog new tricks and you have a new dog. Yet the traditional Japanese values have not disappeared. Though layer upon layer of new sediment is dropped on top of them, they remain bedrock. And surely these traditional values are alien to Western liberalism? Here it must be admitted that the answer is yes. *Half* yes: alien to liberalism, but not to the West, not by a long shot. When at last I understood where I had seen the traditional Japanese values before, and who was their greatest proponent, I laughed and laughed, and I am laughing still. Alien? Non-Western? The man who wrote the book on them was Plato.

63

People who blithely drop phrases about the "Western tradition," meaning virtually all of us, forget that the founders of the liberal social systems were revolutionaries as well as patriarchs. John Locke, the first and still the greatest theorist of both empirical liberalism (science) and political liberalism, set out to overthrow centuries of hallowed metaphysics and to justify the overthrow of unwanted government. It was Locke, followed by Adam Smith and others, who first built the theory of liberal social mechanisms—public processes, like voting or trading or performing experiments, in which no one gets special personal authority (no kings, no dictators, no high priests or oracles) and no one in particular gets to control the outcome. In the liberal scheme of things, no matter who you are your vote is just a vote, your dollar is just a dollar, and your experiment had better work when anyone else tries it. Moreover, there is no last election, last trade, or last hypothesis. America is John Locke's country. It is also Emmanuel Kant's country. Kant codified the liberal sense of justice. Is your action right? Only if anyone else can imitate you without ruining things for everybody. Behavior that is self-defeating when available to everyone is wrong. It is wrong for you to break your promises: if everyone followed your example, then all promises would be disregarded and there would be no gain in promise breaking. So goes the famous Categorical Imperative. If all steal, then stealing can benefit no one because no one has property; if all kill, then killing can benefit no one because all are dead. But if all trade or keep their promises, all can gain: and so trading or keeping promises is all right. In other words, right is right no matter who you happen to be. No special-conduct passes for exalted personages, no hierarchies fixed by moral or divine law. All is right with the world, liberals feel, when we can say: To each according to the same rules. "The sum of all we drive at," says Locke, "is that every man enjoy the same rights that are granted to others." I feel this strongly, for I am a child of the liberal revolution. This, I believe, is why I felt so nervous, so ill at ease and sometimes alarmed, when from time to time I encountered the Platonic public morality that dwells beneath the Lockean social institutions in Japan.

64

One encounters the illiberal old morals on high-school sports teams, with their quasi-military structure and bootcamp rigor and winning-is-everything mindset, their demand for complete submission and unquestioning loyalty. And at the private elementary school where children go virtually naked all through the snowy winter, to make them tough and strong. And in high-school hazings, in which underclassmen are humiliated and bullied on the understanding that they will get their own turn at bullying when they become upper-classmen. And in the ever-present Japanese seniority systems, in which the young suffer and pay their dues and learn to endure and accept and later inflict the same. And on the baseball teams, which often train their players to the point of pain and exhaustion on the grounds that this will build strength of spirit. And at the Suntory beverage company's 1990 beer hall, which used as its design motif the 1936 Berlin Olympics, Hitler's showcase, "known" (said Suntory in its press release) "as the most stoic and masculine" Olympiad. And in the high-school graduation speech in which the principal says, "They say Japanese wood is especially strong.

Do you know why? Because of our hot summers and cold winters. Remember, it is life's hardships that give strength." And in the national university system, with its clear pyramidal hierarchy ranging from Tokyo University on down. And in the government employment system, which assures that all but a fraction of the best elite-ministry jobs go to the graduates of Tokyo University. And especially in the terror of uncontrolled change that still haunts so many Japanese.

65

The bully-worshiping portion of Japan is only one sector of the rich and diverse Japanese moral geography. Yet I was not in Japan a week before this sector had drawn my attention and seduced me with its vaguely fascist magnetism, much as the crocodiles and rattlesnakes charm children at the zoo. As it happened, I had been recently reading Plato, and when I saw the traditional Japanese values—strength through suffering, strength through hierarchy, strength through individual submersion in the group—I recognized what I beheld. "Athens versus Sparta," I thought. "Is that not the metaphor?"

66

Plato's great tract *The Republic* is his treatise on justice: his statement of what constitutes the good society, and when one can feel that all is right with the world. His utopia draws heavily on the Sparta of his day—the opposite pole

from Plato's own cosmopolitan Athens. The good Republic
is a society in which everyone knows his place in a hierarchy graded from top to bottom; at the head is the wise
and benevolent philosopher, and below him is a Guardian
(that is, an administrative-bureaucratic) class; the whole
regime is legitimized by a system of propaganda lies; children
are taken from their parents and assigned their place in the
hierarchy; the young of the Guardian class are taught to be
tough and loyal and enduring in the face of hardship, so as
to make the Republic strong and virtuous; even music and
arts are to be carefully regulated against softening influ-
ences; but these and other sacrifices of personal freedom add
to the harmony and strength of the whole, and so are all to
the good. "My law," says Plato (in the Laws), "will be made
with a general view to the best interests of society at large...,
as I rightly hold the single person and his affairs of minor
importance." No finer statement of the Japanese collectivist
ethic could be imagined, nor of the ethic that seeks group
harmony through finely calibrated hierarchy. Plato speaks
lovingly of the militarized society, of "the habit of never
so much as thinking to do one single act apart from one's
fellows, of making life, to the very uttermost, an unbroken
consort, society, and community of all with all." And why
trouble with so intricate an arrangement of hierarchies and
regulations and lies? Partly out of Plato's native admiration
for discipline and strength and toughness; partly because a

society organized under a philosopher-ruler would have a certain obvious appeal to a philosopher; perhaps mostly, as Karl Popper has so memorably argued, because Plato loathed and feared change, which he saw as decay and decadence from an original universal perfection. The just society would be the one that preserved its strength and integrity against all ravages of change and time. Justice, then, would be that state of affairs in which everyone does well what is appropriate to him—meaning a state in which everyone knows his place and does his duty, down through the generations. This is all, of course, redolent of feudalism, in which each takes his place in the Great Chain of Being, pledging loyalty to the one above and looking after the one below. It is also redolent of Confucianism, with its emphasis on hierarchy and proper place. Confucianism, as everyone tirelessly points out, is where many of the traditional Japanese values came from. But the idea that these values are somehow outside the compass of Western thought is only to be laughed at. The ethical code of Japan's seventeenth-century Tokugawa dictatorship agrees as well with Plato as with Confucius, maybe better. G.B. Sansom describes the feudal Tokugawa code in the following way: "It dwells not upon the pursuit of happiness but upon the unquestioning performance of duties. Loyalty and obedience are its watchwords, and it allows no freedom of thought. In a society so governed every man has his appointed place; in principle none can leave the station in which he was born. It is a minutely regulated hierarchical structure, designed to continue from generation to generation, and in it there is implicit no idea of progress." Here is the Republic indeed. No one would have admired the traditional Japanese values more than Plato, who would have seen in them the gleaming Sparta of his dreams.

67

Europe's traditional values were smashed by revolution; my own country was born as a newfangled experiment; but in Japan you can still find windows, albeit fewer every day, through which to see past corporate modernity to an older sense of justice. I felt initially, until I began to take the country for granted, a kind of privileged fascination. Nowhere are the traditional values and the new institutions, the justice of Plato and the social mechanisms of Locke, wedded so incompatibly and thus so fruitfully as in Japan. The two centuries in which Japan was run by a dynastic military dictatorship on Platonic principles of hierarchy and central regulation inevitably left their deep mark. While John Locke was arguing for the people's right to replace or depose a bad government, the shoguns' closed-door policy kept their subjects sealed off from the winds of liberalism. After the Americans arrived and the shogunate was toppled in the Meiji Restoration of the middle nineteenth century, the feudal past was built upon rather than repudiated. Even today, the Athenian metropolis of modern Tokyo still follows the contours of the Spartan ground below.

68

When one of the windows onto the feudal past opens before him, an American is liable to be shocked. One day I met an American woman who taught English composition at a Japanese women's college. After assigning some readings on discrimination, she asked her students to write essays about it. A number of them replied that this was impossible for them, since they had never experienced discrimination and so could not understand how it felt. Imagine her amazement: in Japan, less than in even the very recent past but considerably more than in America, women are second-class citizens. Many of them now work, but that means they have two jobs, the one at the office and the one at home—for whatever else she may be, a woman is a housewife no matter what. Outside their traditional sphere, women are nowadays typically allowed entry but often not taken seriously. One day when I was giving a speech, a young woman in the front row—one of a very few women in a room full of men—spoke up to ask a question. It was a perfectly good question, perfectly appropriate. To my chagrin, as she spoke many of the men openly laughed at her, tittering the way people do when a child wanders into a grown-ups' meeting and says something cute. In Sapporo I met a woman professor who has worked on both sides of the

Pacific. She said she gets tense and even sick in Japan from the strain of the constant skirmishes she has to fight against her gossiping and resentful male colleagues. I said it sounded just like home. She retorted that in the United States she is known by her work rather than her sex. In Japan a few women work in the elite, but most still work for it, many of them as office ladies, O.L.s, the ubiquitous, chirpy-cute tea-servers. On TV commercials and in service jobs the Japanese woman is Helium Voice: a babytalking child-mother who speaks in a piping squeak that one would have thought unattainable without a surgeon's help. Many Japanese women instinctively cup the hand over the mouth when smiling, so as not to show teeth: the Japanese veil. No wonder, then, that my American acquaintance was astonished. How could her students be so blind as to believe they had never experienced discrimination? Americans are provincial that way. They do not understand that for the more traditional majority of Japanese women—as, indeed, for the most conservative of American women—there was no discrimination to see. Liberal values see unfairness where people play by different rules depending on who they are. Hierarchic values see unfairness when someone is doing what is not appropriate for a person of his type and station. The American teacher's puzzled students would not expect a woman to do what a man would do, any more than they would expect a lamb to do what a lion would do. (Is it "unfair" that lions eat zebra but lambs do not?)

Sometimes people say that the traditional Japanese values entail no notion of fairness, but this is wrong. They simply do not entail the *liberal* notion of fairness, in which particular persons are interchangeable. What is fair depends on who you are and where you are positioned. I became angry because the Japanese would buy me meals without giving me a chance to reciprocate. When I complained that if everyone behaved this way, no one could show hospitality, the answer always amounted to this: But you *wouldn't* behave this way, because you are from a different country and now you are in Japan. Our positions are different, and what is the point of imagining that they are not? So much for the Categorical Imperative. After a while I ceased to be angry and began to accept lunch. After a while they began letting me buy it.

69

A portraitist looking for flaws in his work holds it up to the mirror and sees it afresh, subtly changed, slightly but revealingly. In the Japanese mirror I saw loyalty afresh. We children of liberalism live in a world of depersonalized institutions. We have friends and enemies, some of us are loyal and some are not, but that is business of our own, not the ethical business of the society as a whole. In practice, of course, America is not as different from Japan as we might like to think. All countries have hierarchies—clubs, corporations, fraternities—that are held together by ties of loyalty, though in America we see all of these as faintly disreputable. In our families and our businesses and so many other places we rely on personal loyalty, and so we always will. But we no longer think of loyalty as a social institution. It has entered the realm of the private. This is an enormous change, when you think about it. The death of feudalism came with the notion that one's first loyalty belongs not to a man but to a set of rules. Outside, perhaps, of the inner circle of my family, there is no man or woman, no president or priest, whom I would fight and die for. But I would willingly give my life for the U.S. Constitution, which is a set of rules. This is second nature to me.

70

Not, however, to the Japanese. The traditional values retain their strength most hardily where loyalty is concerned. It would not occur to most Japanese to die for an idea. Fifty years ago they went to die for their emperor; even today, I believe, most people would be far likelier to sacrifice heroically for a boss or a beloved public figure than for a process or a rule. A man told me a strange story. "One foggy night several years ago I was walking, quite alone, down a typical narrow street among the crammed residential buildings of Shinjuku Ward. Alongside the street was a long high wall, the wall around a police station or police operations center. At the end of the wall was a booth where a single policeman sat watching and guarding the wall. As I approached, I noticed that he had his back to me and was absorbed in writing with his finger on the fogged glass at the rear of the booth. I wanted to ask him directions, so I came up close, close enough to read what he was so intently writing. As I looked over his shoulder I could make out the characters for *ten'no*, emperor, on the glass. I spoke to him and he, caught and surprised, immediately broke out of his reverie and turned to me, being very curt to cover his embarrassment. Every time I see a policeman, especially the conservative brutish-looking types, I think of this man, wistfully writing *ten'no* on the fogged glass."

71

Loyalty remains, in Japan, a social institution—not surreptitiously, as in America and Europe, but explicitly. People in Japan rely on their friends to get things done. So do Americans; we call our useful friends the old-boy network. But the Japanese rely on it even to do formal public business. If U.S. government officials want private companies to do something, they file suit or seek legislation or put a notice in the *Federal Register* and "initiate rulemaking." If officials of Japan's Ministry of International Trade and Industry want private companies to do something, they call up their friends in business and ask for a favor. Americans who want to change things think about reforming systems; Japanese tend to think about changing relationships. One day an

American, who had lived and worked in Japan for some time, was telling me about his recent change of bosses. He startled me by remarking in passing that his loyalty was in the process of shifting. Odd, I thought. Anyone's loyalty would shift, yes; but ordinarily you would not hear an American talk that way. Americans usually talk as though a job is a job and one's loyalty is to one's paycheck. In Japan, it is by and large the loyalty that is constant and the paycheck that is incidental. The loyalty outlasts, in a sense, even the one who pledges it. The human being passes but the bonds of loyalty last forever. The political scientist Takeshi Ishida cites the case of an executive who killed himself in 1979 when his company, whose secrets he knew, was caught in scandal. "He committed suicide and took these secrets to the grave forever. According to the newspapers, he left a note in which he wrote, 'The company is eternal. It is our duty to devote our lives to that eternity. Our employment may last for only twenty or thirty years, but the life of the company is eternal. I must be brave and act as a man to protect that eternal life.'"

72

Young workers, fresh from high school or college and as yet unattached except to family, used to pledge their fealty to a company much as a vassal or a retainer would to his lord, and the bond was supposed to be eternal. (Not that it always was. In medieval Japan, people switched sides all the time. As for modern Japan, according to the social psychologist Sumiko Iwao the average stay at a single company has been in the range of a dozen years or so—longtime employment, not lifetime employment.) In recent years people have begun to switch jobs more often and more openly. Magazines have popped up for new-job seekers; Japan's leading newspaper, the *Asahi Shimbun*, has (an editor there told me) taken to advertising openly for experienced writers from other publications, whereas in the past such steals were always arranged through back channels. One day I was riding in a car with a few young bureaucrats of one of the prefectural governments. I was talking to a thirty-year-old. It turned out that he had once worked for one of the renowned corporations in Tokyo, putting in the standard days that stretched from eight in the morning till ten or eleven at night; but he felt hollow and quit, just like that, to go backpacking around Japan and learn what's really important. For more than a year he lived off his savings and worked itinerantly, finding jobs despite the suspicion which in Japan always attaches itself to the unattached. The man in the front seat—he was thirty-two— had been listening to the story. He turned around and said that he too had quit his big-company job in Tokyo, fleeing to the calmer waters of local government. The new values are gaining, inch by inch.

73

Yet it remains broadly true that personal attachment and personal loyalty define the self in Japan, even at the level of national decision making. We Americans are used to thinking of politicians as vehicles for their policies. We vote not merely for a particular person but for a "conservative" or a "liberal," based on "litmus tests" and "the record." Americans vote also on "character," but this we talk about as "the character issue," the issue being whether the candidate is of sturdy enough character to set sensible policies. Japanese voters are more used to thinking of politicians as personages, personalities, who might or might not be worthy of loyalty. It becomes extremely important for Japanese politicians to attend or acknowledge weddings, meet constituents, send flowers or gifts on special occasions, and otherwise show how much they care. The voter tends to see his representatives as useful not because they were elected—anyone can be elected—but because they are personally attached to him. Me, I would resent being "represented" by a politician who was not properly elected, however loyal to me he might be. I suspected that many Japanese voters, by contrast, would dislike being represented by a politician who was not loyal to them, no matter how large a majority he polled. Although this attitude is decidedly illiberal, in that it elevates persons above process, it is not crazy. The Japanese traditional values recall a truth from which liberalism averts its eyes. Relationships

are power. They cannot be codified, they are not accountable, you cannot hire lawyers or consultants to manage them
for you. But, no less than rules, relationships work for those
who use them well. Japanese politicians, understanding as
much, are known at times to appeal flagrantly to people's
feelings. In elections in the countryside, an effective vote-
getting technique is to plead pathetically, preferably with
a great show of sincerity and even tears. In Hokkaido, the
northern island, one candidate in 1989 brought his aged
father to a campaign appearance. The father ostentatiously
sobbed that all he wanted before he died was to see his son
become a congressman. This went over boffo. In America,
such politicking would probably not work even in Louisiana;
only the insane or desperate would try it, namely Richard
Nixon in the famous Checkers speech. The tactic's success in
Japan, however, is not as absurd as one might initially think.
By doing a candidate a personal favor, the voters establish
that he owes them. Never mind his policies: he will be loyal.
Partly the personalization of politics bespeaks a peculiarity
of the Japanese electoral system, which pits members of the
same party against each other in every legislative district and
so makes voting on the issues very difficult. But partly it
bespeaks a certain subterranean truth in the bus attendant's
wisdom about his country. Japan mates liberal public systems
with illiberal public values. Above ground you see the liberal
metropolis. But below are the traditional values. Dig—you

must dig deeper every year—and you will find the underground springs of Platonic hierarchic collectivism. In that sense the bus attendant was not wrong when he said: "It's a feudal system based on personal relationships."

74

Or rather the system is, said two Japanese friends of mine, roaring with laughter, a giant can of asparagus. We were getting drunk, the newspaperman, the legal-affairs department man, and I. The newspaperman was white-haired and eloquent in English, his colleague was younger and quieter. We were sitting in one of Tokyo's small yakitori restaurants, we had lost count of our drinks, and gradually everything was becoming clear. At last we attained a state of divine clarity in which we understood Japanese society. Inspiration had seized the legal-affairs man. You have to imagine, he was saying, a can of asparaguses. (In Japanese English, "asparagus" has a plural form—another useful Japanese innovation.) Each of the more than a dozen asparaguses is a division of his company—this company being one of Japan's most powerful. Each division hires kids out of college and moves them up through the ranks. At the point of each asparagus is the division director. Major policy decisions, such as expansion plans or austerity measures, are made by consensus among the most powerful directors; but the people just above the middle level, two-thirds of the way up, are the ones who make the bulk of the daily decisions. People communicate up and down each asparagus. Sideways communication goes on too, between people of the same seniority (members of the same class), though this is less formal. And what about the guy at the top, the president of the company, I asked—what does he do? He sings karaoke, came the reply; and through the beery haze I understood this as a reference to one of Japan's tackiest and pleasantest customs, wherein people drinking together entertain each other and let their hair down by singing popular songs to prerecorded accompaniment. The guy at the top was chosen for being unobjectionable to everybody else and for being able to "sing" soothingly to employees and clients. So who is accountable? Everyone and no one. Isn't this frustrating? Oh, no, on the contrary. This is the way we middle-level people like things. We are left alone to do our jobs, as long as we are careful to consult up and down the hierarchy, and as long as through our classmates we watch out for trouble.

75

In the old days of the shogunate, an adviser who advocated a policy that failed was expected to redeem his honor by disemboweling himself. Understandably, this led to a certain reluctance to take responsibility. So the traditional hierarchism was modified away from the classic Western authoritarian model and toward the Japanese asparagus model. In the economic sector, of course, the spears of asparagus are the great companies. In the Diet, they are the political parties and, within the ruling Liberal Democratic Party, the so-called factions: clubs whose members are bound together, not by loyalty to particular policies or ideas, but by loyalty to one of several charismatic, empire-building faction chiefs. In the government bureaucracy, the asparagus spears are the ministries, each headed by an appointed minister whose power is greatly circumscribed in practice by the vast career bureaucracy beneath him. The guy on top, in principle, is the prime minister. The prime minister in 1990, however, exemplified the reality: Toshiki Kaifu was chosen for being unobjectionable to everybody else, and for singing good karaoke to his party members and to the American president. Various observers have pointed out that the asparagus system is (as Masao Maruyama has put it) a "system of irresponsibility," or that it behaves responsibly but that no one within it is held accountable. "Even after the horrors of the mass murders of Nanking, the indiscriminate bombing of Manila and all the other excesses of the Pacific war," writes the brilliant scholar and critic Shuichi Kato, "Japanese society did not seek out one individual on whom to pin the blame. Rather it accepted collective responsibility. . . . [I]ndividual responsibility is not accepted as a concept." A fair complaint, but buck passing is endemic in every society. In the American savings and loan debacle—a world-class financial collapse caused largely by government neglect and folly—politicians responded to the crisis by scrambling frantically to move the blame somewhere else. Everyone sang karaoke about how the responsibility belonged to everybody and thus nobody. Ronald Reagan, who discovered that assessing blame is easier than accepting responsibility, made a career of blaming liberals, blaming Democrats, blaming Congress, blaming Jimmy Carter. Smile and smile, blame and blame. True, in America buck passing is generally seen as craven. In Japan it is appreciated as consensus building—which, of course, it is. You build a consensus by giving everybody a piece of the decision, and so spreading blame around. Buck passing is also a way to fuzz disagreement and to make the group rather than the individual the basic unit of social decision making. To me the surprising thing was how socially productive passing the buck can be, as long as the buck passers are under enough pressure to behave responsibly. If I were faced with the choice, I would rather work in my legal-affairs man's company than in one of the American kind where an autocratic nincompoop flushes his company and workers down the toilet but is later—maybe—held accountable to the stockholders. Buck passing has its virtues.

76

True, in an asparagus system it is always better to be at the top of the asparagus than at the bottom. Ask any peasant or army private or junior salesman. In Japan the junior people spend their first five years doing the moral equivalent of latrine duty. Still more true, though, is this: best of all is not to be outside the can.

77

"The underdog finds no friend in Japan," Donald Richie has written. "Rather, it takes a sentimental culture, such as ours, to find some virtue in being weak." Ours? No: many Americans feel a certain friendly sympathy for the underdog, but we are no different from the Japanese in worshiping success and celebrating the "winner." No one who has been to Texas—home of the Dallas Cowboys, "America's Team" until they started losing—could say otherwise. The difference is not in personal attitudes but in social institutions. To me one of the most attractive features, and inevitably also one of the most frustrating, of the American system is that it fairly bristles with external points of access. We have created a million ways for the outsider, even the solitary one, to mount a challenge. You do not need to be on the inside to get results; you only need a lawyer. In our politics, if you do not like the government's policy you can try getting new regulations written, and if regulators turn you away you can write to your congressman, and if your congressman ignores your letter you can hire a lobbyist, and if the lobbyist gets no results you can sue, and if your suit fails you can appeal, and if at length your appeals are exhausted, you can try pressing some new strategy at some other level of government, and if all else fails you can try to vote the bastards out. There are more doors than anyone could possibly keep shut, and if you find one door unpromising, you just try another. When we regulate, we require first that all proposals be announced publicly, then publicly commented upon, then vetted through a series of federal offices, then (sometimes) approved by Congress and (often) tested in court. When we pass laws, we hold hearings and insist that they be public. In our intellectual system, we insist that in principle a hypothesis be open to testing by anybody at any time, and that sources and rationales be as openly displayed as conclusions. The most powerful and perfect theory in all of science, Newtonian mechanics, was upended by an obscure patent examiner (named Einstein). Our economic system offers somewhat less recourse, but if your situation becomes intolerable you can usually change jobs or find some alternative, and you can always get yourself a lawyer and make someone else's life miserable, which is why there are nineteen times as many lawyers per capita in the United States as in Japan. We do not especially love the underdog in America, but we give him a crowbar and plenty of cracks at which to pry.

78

I went to watch a committee of Japanese legislators set the

budget for the Ministry of International Trade and Industry. It looked very much like an American congressional committee meeting—so much so that I am hesitant to spend the next few sentences harping on the major point of difference. But that point is important: the Japanese committee meeting was not open to the public. You had to be someone or know someone to get inside. This is because it was a meeting, not of the Diet, but of a policy-making committee of the Liberal Democratic Party. Well, a political party is private, and so for the Liberal Democrats to regard their meetings as internal business is wholly legitimate. Yet it is a fact that, because the Liberal Democratic Party has been in power for most of the postwar era, its decisions are the ones that count—and they are made in private, literally in smoke-filled rooms. In Japan it is never easy for the outsider or the unattached to mount a challenge, because the points of external access are few, and if you use them you are considered a troublemaker or an eccentric. Nor are you likely to have much success. Suppose you are a young member of the Diet and you are fed up with the existing policies. You want to challenge the bureaucracy's decisions. But your office consists, in its entirety, of two rooms, each barely bigger than a closet; your government-paid staff in Tokyo consists of two desperately overworked aides. (A friend of mine once asked a Diet member why members of the legislature did not vote themselves more staff, as their American counterparts have done ad infinitum. Because, he replied definitively, we don't have enough space for any more staff. The diabolically clever follow-up—why don't you vote yourselves more office space?—completely stumped the poor man.) You have no investigative subcommittee or Government Accountability Office or Congressional Budget Office, and so you rely on the bureaucracy for information. You cannot go around it. Moreover, the bureaucracy and the leadership of your party and faction are careful to stay on each other's good side and to keep each other's bread buttered. If you want to change the party's policy, you must wait patiently perhaps twenty years, until you attain a high place in the legislative pecking order. By then you won't want to change the policy. If you were an American faced with these options, you might run for president, and so try to establish an independent base of influence; but in Japan, because the system is parliamentary, the prime minister is always chosen from among the senior Diet members. If you were an American, you might quit the Diet and run for governor, using the state as your platform; and so some Japanese, such as Governor Morihiro Hosokawa of Kumamoto (formerly a Diet member), have indeed done; but you would soon find that seventy percent of your prefectural budget comes from Tokyo, where it is channeled through the bureaucracy. Governors, even mayors, must constantly shuttle to Tokyo as supplicants, and Governor Hosokawa says that in recent decades the centralization has tended, if anything, to increase. Checkmate.

79

You can find instances of this kind throughout Japan: in the press clubs, the distribution system, everywhere. Japanese social institutions spent hundreds of years assiduously cutting off and plugging alternative channels of any kind. The legacy is that to this day there are precious few platforms from which the independent-minded or the malcontent can challenge any of the big bureaucracies, public or private. To get things done you must build relationships, earn loyalty, develop trust, and pay your dues. You must, in other words, get inside. If you are a farmer or a retailer, you had better work through the established distribution network, or else you had better be prepared for a long slog uphill. If you are a politician, you had better wait your turn before you start making waves. The Japanese guard relationships—relationships are power—as jealously as liberals guard rules; new entrants upset old and comfortable relationships; and so Japanese society presents itself as a thicket of obstacles to new entry. Japan is the insiders' paradise, the stakeholders' dictatorship. God help the newcomer, for the Japanese won't.

80

Especially savory are the moments when someone turns on the lights and the insiders are caught with their pants down, doing the wrong sorts of favors for each other. In such instances you can always win if you bet that: the scandal will involve fat cats cutting deals to the exclusion of little guys, outsiders, and newcorners; the existence of the deal will have been publicly denied but privately widely acknowledged; somebody senior will issue a public apology and resign (an improvement, I think, over the American system, where wrongdoing is denied long after it has become undeniable and where everyone demands the resignation of somebody else); government officials will express the deepest regret and announce that such a thing will not happen again; such a thing will happen again. Not long ago someone turned on the lights and the world's biggest brokerage house, Nomura Securities Company, admitted that it had secretly been reimbursing its largest customers for their stock market losses. This amounted to a kind of sure-fire investment deal for the blessed big shots, and it was of necessity paid for by the company's smaller and foreign accounts, who were not similarly favored. "In its stunning announcement," said the *New York Times*, "Nomura reversed a heated denial that it made just one day earlier and confirmed reports that it had made nearly $120 million in such payments. . . . Clearly embarrassed by the disclosures, the Vice Minister of Finance, Hiroshi Yasuda, was quoted today as expressing 'great regret' over the situation. Mr. Yasuda added that the ministry would tighten its controls over securities companies. But the warning was met with some skepticism in the industry because the government has tolerated such practices for so long." So embarrassing! So delectable!

81

The system looks terrible on paper, I know. Yet anybody who comes to Japan and looks about will, if he is honest with himself, acknowledge that there is a benevolent side as well—an enviable side. Whether you find Japan disgusting or admirable will depend to a very great degree on whether you look mainly at processes or at outcomes. If you look at processes, then, like the Dutch writer Karel van Wolferen, you will see Japan as a shadowy power game rigged by conniving insiders. If you look at outcomes, then you will see a nation that has attained what most societies merely aspire to: wealth, security, stability, peace. To outsiders, the Japanese way, with its traded favors and smoke-filled rooms and bureaucratic monopolies, looks shady and even dirty; yet there is no denying that it produces one of the world's few genuinely decent societies. You feel the decency in the quiet residential lanes; you feel it in the shopping districts, and in the mom-and-pop stores that sell everything from fruit to videocassette recorders in tiny quantities. When the shampoo runs out, the store sends a boy out for ten more bottles. The owners of these little shops (which account for more than half of all retail sales) are organized, they are established, and they are insiders; hence they have received legal protection from larger and more efficient competitors; hence Japanese consumers pay higher prices than they otherwise would. Yet many consumers support the small-store protectionism.

They say they like the good service and personal warmth in the little stores, which are indeed much less antiseptic than Kmart and Sears. Once I asked a man why anyone would buy a TV at the neighborhood electronics shop, where prices were exorbitant and selection was thin. He replied that he bought his own TV there because if it broke the shop would fix it for free and meanwhile lend him a new one. Garden-variety American that I am, with my garden-variety American "buts," I would always say: but if people like these small stores so much, they will continue to shop there, even after the laws are liberalized and bigger stores are allowed— just give consumers the choice. We Americans think that choice is something that you cannot have too much of. The average Japanese is more likely to deny himself, and others, choices in order to curtail change and so preserve the web of comfortable existing relationships. He loses something in the bargain, but he also gains something—if, I mean, he is on the inside, and so in a position to capture benefits. I chafe at the Japanese way, but I was forced to admit that my own attitude toward newcomers— the more newcomers, the better—is at bottom a prejudice. (Though I think it is the right prejudice.) I was also forced to admit that I felt at home amid the charm of the small shops and their friendly owners, and that I too would hate to see them go. Until I came to Tokyo, I had never known the joys of small-town life.

82

In Japan I remembered: I was walking in Jerusalem, near the central bus terminal. I passed a young man, about twenty years old and sandy-blond, sitting cross-legged on the ground and holding a sign asking for money. I was surprised by the sight of a begging young foreigner (British, it turned out), so I stood nearby and watched for a minute while I decided whether to strike up a conversation. As I stood there an Israeli man approached him and knelt down. Do you need work, can you paint? Yes? Then come to this address Sunday and you have a job. The young man accepted. No sooner had the first man left than a second appeared. Do you need a place to stay? Come to my kibbutz. (The young man had been traveling, I found out when I finally approached him, and had run out of money.) I stood on the corner and tried to recall when I had last seen anyone offer a job or a bed to such a person in America. I am still trying to recall.

83

But this sort of thing happens in a small island nation: by which I mean not a nation which is really an island (Israel is not) or which is really small (Japan is not), but a nation that takes its identity from a sense of common vulnerability in a hostile or indifferent world. Israel, in that sense, is a small island nation, and Jews (the insiders) in Israel look after each other in a way that is both oppressive and sublime. So also with Japan. Not long ago an opinion poll asked Japanese and Americans whether their countries were liked or disliked in the world. The Americans, by margins of about two to one, said that America is liked and also that Japan is liked. The Japanese, by a margin of better than two to one, said that the United States is liked, but by a margin almost as great they said that Japan is disliked. *Wareware nihonjin*, we Japanese, are so few, so alike, so mistrusted: we must stick together.

84

The Japanese will always tell you that they live in a small island nation. This is said so often in Japan as to be for practical purposes a single word. It is, with "homogeneity," one of the two explanations for everything. One day I asked an official of the Education Ministry why it was necessary, in the 1990s, to have a bureau whose business was to ensure that all public schools are alike. Because, he said, we are a small island nation. The Tokyo police ran an antispeeding campaign a few years ago, using the catchphrase, "Japan's so small, why are you driving so fast?" Of course the truth is that Japan is a very large island nation, poor in natural resources but rich in everything else. But never mind: the attitude is its own reality. You often meet Japanese who are determined not to notice that their country's population numbers 125 million and that its gross national product is the world's second largest. An American diplomat I know was in the city of Sendai giving an interview to an editor from the local newspaper. The diplomat was asked where he had been stationed before Japan. He replied that he had served in Finland (population: 5 million) and in New Zealand (population: 3.3 million, and 58 million sheep). "Oh," said the journalist, "I see the pattern." The startled diplomat asked: "What's the pattern?" And the editor replied: "You prefer to work in small countries." See? Finland, New Zealand, Japan.

85

It can be infuriating and suffocating, living in a small island nation, for there is no escape from others, and you are required to be accommodating even when you have been wronged. You find this in Israel, in Japan, and in small-town America. Donald Richie writes of being driven to move out of his apartment by the crazy old woman downstairs, who endlessly complained that he made loud noises. In fact, he did no such thing; the noises were all in her head. The other neighbors knew that he was a quiet tenant, and the police did, too, but they all advised him to try to be even quieter, saying, "Japan's a small country. We all have to get on peacefully together somehow." Andy Griffith might say something like that as he sought to keep the peace in Mayberry. (Barney Fife would noisily demand justice.) He might echo the woman of Minamata, who took no action against the man who pushed her: "That is the meaning of a communal way of living."

86

Yet the people of Mayberry felt the way a Jew feels in Israel or the way a Japanese feels among the small shops and clubby relationships: supported, protected, cocooned. One feels, in Japan, that one can get lost anywhere and still be looked after, even though this is not literally the case. One day in a sushi bar I watched as a man's coat fell from the back of his chair. Without a word to anybody, a woman waiting behind him neatly replaced the coat, just the way it had been. The man never knew that he had either needed help or received it. I discovered that if I were pressed to give a single word which I associated with Japan, the word would be: *cozy*. Cozy relationships, cozy deals, cozy lives—coziness as a national aspiration. Even I, the foreigner, was folded in the security blanket, and I liked it. This is not to say that I would trade in my citizenship. I believe I prefer the sharp edges of American society to the heavy weight of the Japanese. But I cannot pretend that the other choice is unappealing. One week alone when I was in Japan, three children in New York were killed as random victims of bullets and a fourth was wounded critically.

87

Like my friend the editorial writer, who always said, "I feel strongly both ways," I was divided against myself for a long time. It was, as I have mentioned, not that my picture of

Japan was confused or chaotic, particularly; it was that there were two of them, and they didn't fit together. I went back and forth. Among other foreigners I found polarization to a degree that was altogether unsettling. Most people either love or hate New York City, but each party understands why the other feels as it does. I detest the subways, but it is easy for me to see why you love the Met. In the case of people reacting to Japan—Japanese as well as foreign—the divide is similarly wide, but communications across it are out. In the debate about Japan, each side is a little astounded by the incomprehension of the other. A senior Foreign Ministry man was at a loss to understand how Americans could regard his country as dangerous or as less liberal than other major industrial democracies; yet it was the Japanese bus attendant who had grumbled about the "feudal" society, and it was the intellectually inclined (and so frustrated) young Japanese salaryman who told me that the worst is really true—the people around him are numbed sheep.

88

What is true elsewhere, I concluded at last, is true of Japan: where you stand, and what you see, depends on where you sit. But because in Japan it matters so much whether you are inside or out, and whether you *feel* yourself to be inside or out, the differentness of view is especially pronounced. In Japan, even more than in America, success is defined as membership in the Ichi-ban Club—the Top Club, the number-one asparagus, the Ministry of Finance or the Mitsubishi Corporation or Tokyo University. If you are in the Ichi-ban Club, the skids are greased for you. You will have a prosperous career and many good social contacts. You will be, in effect, a leading Rotarian in small-town America. Things will work for you. If you are in a low-ranking club, it will be harder for you to get what you want. (This, of course, is true also in America or anywhere else.) And if you are an outsider, you will run into spongy walls again and again. Gradually I came to see that the two pictures of Japan do fit together, are indeed the same picture. What did not fit together were the observers.

89

How You See Japan, or
Where You Stand Depends on Where You Sit

Insiders *Ichi-ban Club;* *"Handlers"*	Outsiders *Japanese and Foreign;* *"Bashers"*
Democratic	Bureaucratic/administrative state
Liberal	Feudal/hierarchic
Open	Closed
Free	"Free"
Flexible	Rigid
Fast-changing	Static, never really changes
Benign	Nervous-making, threatening, sinister
Patient	Intractable
Gentle	Insidious
Steady	Unpredictable, volatile
Misunderstood	Misunderstood

Part Two

90

There I should leave matters. It is dishonest to choose: one must simply accept that Japan is liberal but also feudal, open but also closed, free but also "free." Almost fifty years ago, in her landmark study *The Chrysanthemum and the Sword*, the cultural anthropologist Ruth Benedict wrote: "During the past seventy-five years since Japan's closed doors were opened, the Japanese have been described in the most fantastic series of 'but also's' ever used for any nation in the world." Other countries, too, have their "but also's." America is socially mobile but also class-bound, internationalist but also self-obsessed and provincial, and so on. America, however, gives you handles. It tags itself as the country that stands for democracy, liberty, individualism, and the rest; and observers are encouraged to think that if they know the tags they understand the society. Thus the Japanese, like other foreigners, believe they understand America because they know it is "individualistic" and "multiracial." They, by contrast, live in a place where grand ideological theory has never been much indulged in or appreciated as an art form, and so they give you no such ready-made handles. There are no sentences you can master in order to feel you understand Japan. Therefore in the ocean of "but also's" you must simply swim.

91

There I should leave matters, yes: but there I cannot. One must conclude about Japan; for Japan is now, in all ways but militarily, the world's second-greatest power, and growing stronger. Together Japan and the United States account for more than forty percent of the world's economic output. The elephant is now very big indeed, big enough to shift the scales, big enough to upset everything. To the extent that we outsiders need to know what to expect of the creature and where it will put its weight, "but also" will not do.

92

In trying to figure out what to do about a foreign power, Americans rightly ask as the first question: Is this nation's social system or way of life so deeply inimical to ours that its very existence is a threat? Must the regime be contained, or, if possible, changed, or, if necessary, destroyed? In the case of the Soviet Union, for many years the answer was yes; yes also in the case of Botha's South Africa and Khomeini's Iran and Kim's North Korea. Some countries—Saudi Arabia—are right on the border. Japan is not on the border. It is not, in my opinion, even close. It is no more a moral threat than Germany.

93

The next question, then, is the narrower and more temporal one: Is the country's current policy drift a threat to American interests? Does or will the country use its power in ways that hurt the United States or the world, either by design or by accident? This question is entirely legitimate, and it is the focus of the big argument about Japan today. People who say the answer is yes have come to be lumped together under the brainless rubric "revisionist," despite the fact that their views on specifics are very different. Whether they are right or wrong in their conclusions, they have raised the important question. I will try to give an answer.

94

My good fortune was to be in Japan when a series of talks with the United States, known as the Structural Impediments Initiative, was completed. If Japan's economy is reminiscent of America's in the days of the great trusts and company towns, then in the Structural Impediments Initiative the Americans were playing the part of the turn-of-the-century trustbusters. Americans pressed for liberalization of the Large Retail Stores Law, on the grounds that the protection for small shops perpetuated an antiquated distribution system that was hard for newcomers (read: Americans) to penetrate; they pressed for a commitment to enforce existing Japanese antitrust law, on the grounds that the cartels had sewn up markets and combined to make life difficult for those outside the club (read: Americans); and so on. On those points and others like them the Americans won concessions; and within proud sovereign Japan, the reaction was astonishing. Newspaper editorials hailed the foreign meddling, correctly, as a boon to long-suffering Japanese consumers. The *Nihon Keizai Shimbun* said: "...the U.S. demands uphold the interests of Japan's consumers in general . . . more positively than any political party of Japan." *Chunichi Shimbun/Tokyo Shimbun* syndicate: "The external pressure being applied in the course of the SII talks will provide a good opportunity to carry out democratic reform of the economy. . . ." *Sankei Shimbun*: ". . . the great majority of the Japanese people wish to see the proposals implemented. . . ." *Hokkai Times*: ". . . the political power structure of Japan is incapable of carrying out self-reform, requiring external pressure, to a certain extent, to institute reform." But this was not all. Again and again Japanese people told me, in effect: Keep up the good work, keep up your pressuring and hectoring. Outside pressure, one man told me, making a gesture of pounding his head against something, offers the best chance of "breaking the wall." He did not see what he himself could do that might break it. An American I know was riding in a taxi when the driver turned around and told him, in Japanese: I hope you Americans keep hammering away at us, because nothing else will work. One night over drinks I told an American scholar how much the Japanese reaction had surprised me. He leaned over the table. "What does this tell you?" he asked darkly, and then answered his own question: "It's not a democracy."

95

On a country highway in the richly wooded hills of Oita, on the southern island of Kyushu, I was driving with a youngish professional man. He was telling me about his volunteer work as a local organizer for a Liberal Democratic politician from his district. I had asked him why he—a man with a family, after all—put in so much time. Because you believe in this politician? The response was a derisive snort. I support him, he said, because our region has long had affinities for the opposition parties, and consequently we are out of favor with the Liberal Democrats, and consequently our roads and bridges and public facilities are in the shape you see. He said: If I and others can strengthen the ties to the ruling party, we in Oita can get a bigger slice of the pie. Perhaps—I said—you should do what I might do: work instead to throw the bastards out, and put the fear of God into them. He shook his head. The Liberal Democrats had ruled for thirty-five years and no one could beat them and the opposition was worse anyway, he said. There was no alternative. Therefore it was best not to fight City Hall, but instead to curry favor.

96

I met some small-town mayors and put the question to them point-blank, as only a foreigner can do. One of them was then putting the finishing touches on a local revitalization plan, which included a new resort and the like. If not for your long-nourished connections to the Liberal Democrats, I asked him, could you get money from Tokyo for these development projects? Well, he said, probably not—or maybe, but it wouldn't necessarily be easy. In another town, the mayor broke out the budget. A seventh of the town's money was raised and spent locally. Virtually all the rest came from or through Tokyo. Most of that was dispensed by formula, to ensure fairness. However, public works projects, which accounted for about a quarter of the town budget, required specific approval from the officials in Tokyo. The Tokyo bureaucracy is controlled by the Liberal Democrats. The mayor's partisan affiliation had long been with the—guess who?—Liberal Democrats. And this, he acknowledged, did not hurt.

97

Everyone knows what's going on here: pork-barrel machine politics. It goes on everyplace, emphatically including America, where honest graft has the sort of long and colorful history that attends prostitution and other disreputable institutions that work. Members of the U.S. Congress, Republicans and Democrats indistinguishably, make their living by denouncing federal "big spenders" while boasting about all the bacon they bring home from the federal larder. For two hundred years this has been the sacred principle of American democracy: "The greatest goodies for the greatest number." Because the politicians take their pay in votes rather than in furs and yachts, the system is regarded as distasteful but not quite corrupt, in America and Japan alike. However, there is a difference. In Japan the pork is dispensed by a single-party machine, deeply entrenched and thoroughly in control of the national bureaucracy. Thus when voters grow exasperated their options are few. Americans living in certain big cities, particularly a few decades ago, know exactly what this is like: you can vote for whomever you please, if you don't care whether your trash is picked up. To lubricate the gears, the Japanese politicians raise large sums of money and spread it liberally among local politicians and supporters. And a great deal is spent. In the 1989 electoral fund-raising cycle alone, politicians and political parties collected ¥173 billion, or something like $1.3 billion. Money comes from corporations and fat cats. Sometimes it comes via shakedown ("Gentlemen, I worry that the climate for businesses like yours might suffer in Japan if the opposition makes a lot of headway in the coming elections"), but much more commonly it comes in the form of cash or staff donated willingly to ensure that the political interests of the donors will be looked after. Japan is Mayor Curley's Boston or Mayor Daley's Chicago, or, if you prefer, Mexico with an efficient bureaucracy. Very cozy.

98

Agriculture is the classic example, an extreme case and therefore vividly illustrative. Japanese farming is organized through an intricate system of agricultural cooperatives, known as Nogyo Kyodo Kumiai, or Nokyo. They buy the harvests, sell the farmers seed and fertilizer and insurance, extend credit, and do practically everything else. The thousands of village cooperatives are organized into prefectural associations and above those is the national association. If you are a farmer, you had better work through the Nokyo, for (writes Yujiro Hayami in his 1988 book *Japanese Agriculture under Siege: The Political Economy of Agricultural Policies*) "probably more than 70 percent of the rice and fertilizers is marketed through the agricultural cooperatives." These cooperatives "are designated as sole marketing agents from the farm-gate to the wholesale level and need no major effort to earn large commissions," and their position is strengthened by direct and indirect government backing. It's a company town, in other words. Unfortunately for the farmers, Nokyo sells fertilizer at rates well above international prices, and "no private trader and manufacturer dares to sell fertilizers cheaper than the cartel price for fear of retaliation by Nokyo, which has an overwhelming share in fertilizer marketing." Fortunately for the farmers, Nokyo buys their crop at rates well above the international price. This is possible because farmers are heavily subsidized (even more so than they are in America and Europe), and because they are protected from cheaper imports (though international pressure has been opening the market ever so gradually). Farmers are subsidized and protected because Nokyo acts as a political machine for the Liberal Democratic Party, raising votes and yen by the thousands and millions; and the Liberal Democratic Party is tight with the Agriculture Ministry; and the ministry in turn relies on Nokyo's support to maintain a strong political base and to provide what Hayami calls "lucrative employment opportunities" for bureaucrats when they retire from the ministry. "It is also well known," he says, "that the allocation of agricultural subsidies—especially to land-infrastructure projects of which major beneficiaries are the contractors who often dominate local politics—is a major source of power for both bureaucrats and politicians." The result is that the Liberal Democrats stay in office, the agricultural bureaucracy remains secure, and Nokyo captures and then doles out to its members and supporters monopoly benefits estimated conservatively at over ¥110 billion (with a B) in 1985 alone. A good deal all the way around—unless you happen to be shopping for food in Japan or trying to export your crop to Japan, in which case you are stuck with the bill. It must be said that American agricultural politics differs only in extent, and not in kind: organized farmers, many of them well-to-do, use their political muscle to extract welfare from generally oblivious taxpayers. However, the presence of interlocking monopoly dealers—Nokyo, the ministry, the entrenched ruling party—is a trait which used to be quite characteristic of America but now is much more characteristic of Japan. The pattern is repeated again and again in Japanese politics. A ruling-party clique acts as guardian of the airlines, enabling them to charge fares higher than the international norm. Small shops and giant securities firms use their clout to extract protection and benefits. And so on.

99

So the system is neither exotic nor obscure. Why do the people put up with it? The answers, again, are neither exotic nor obscure.

100

First, because the voters of Japan are indolent and unused to taking charge. For more than forty years—the entire period of stable Japanese democracy—the United States has made the major political decisions for both countries. Before that, the Japanese lived under an imposed constitution, which referred to the people as "subjects." And before the Meiji constitution there was the bureaucratic dictatorship and its feudal values. Even today the old values interfere with the exercise of modern democratic decision making: people still have not quite figured out that they, and not someone above them, are in charge. People I met tended to feel spoken for by their elected officials rather than represented by them. Shoganai. When the people shrugged and said "shoganai" I wanted to grab them by the lapels and shake them, so annoyed did I become. Their attitude combined an utterly defeatist (and so self-fulfilling) cynicism about politics with a bovine unwillingness to assume control.

101

As I wrote the sentences a few paragraphs above, the day's second ground tremor came and went. No damage, but it brought a long holding of breath while everyone waited to see if things would be the same or different afterward. This helps a little to understand. Shoganai. It can't be helped. Traditionally the Japanese, as the political scientist Takeshi Ishida has so insightfully said, have tended to regard social phenomena as natural events. Wars and dictatorships, like droughts and earthquakes, just come and go. You wait them out.

102

Well, I am not being entirely fair to the Japanese. After a while I began to doubt whether, if I were in their shoes today, I would be any less bovine. For the other reason people put up with the City Hall system is that it has delivered. It has always stayed one step ahead of the populist reaction. The Japanese cartelists are smarter than their rapacious counterparts in Tammany Hall America or in OPEC: they understand that if they get too greedy, if they push the public's patience too far, people will begin to circumvent or even rebel, reformers will be swept into power, and then the nice cozy system will crumble. The farmers of Japan, indeed, have been too greedy, and ever so slowly their influence is eroding as opinion shifts toward liberalization. As for the Liberal Democrats, they have been careful not to give out *too* many favors, not to presume *too* much on the voters. American democracy is noisy and fast, with political competitors inventing choices and voters grabbing them. Japanese democracy is quiet and slow, with the ruling party feeling for vibrations in its web and responding when it senses trouble. I was irritated with the people for not making more vibrations. Japan needs but lacks a populist, hang-'em-high political tradition. Yet any competent politician, never mind where, knows one thing if he knows nothing else: peace and prosperity are an unbeatable ticket. And peace and prosperity are what the Japanese City Hall has for forty years concentrated single-mindedly on delivering, with enormous success. One day I was talking to a Japanese man who knows both our countries well. When I asked him why the Japanese put up with so much, he replied without hesitation: "For forty years, things have gotten better here every year." And it's true. The country has stayed out of war and it has risen from rubble to riches in the blink of an eye. Since 1960 the average wage of Japanese workers, after adjusting for inflation, has tripled, a record that American wages cannot come close to matching. The Japanese economy grows at almost twice the rate of the American economy—reliably. Who is going to hang politicians for crimes like those?

103

And so my American friend was wrong. Japan is a democracy—a but-also democracy, perhaps, yet a democracy nonetheless. I would rather live in a democracy that has keen political competition, and I would resent the Japanese insiders' suppression of alternatives. But I have to grant that Mayor Daley's system, dominated by a single party with sensitive antennae, works acceptably well, both in Chicago and in Japan.

104

With, however, one grave reservation, whose full implications are now coming to bear dangerously upon Japan and her allies.

105

Small things are too much dwelt on by writers about Japan, and I am no exception. Japan has been too closely observed. Yet one cannot help noticing the little things. Often, at restaurants, my Japanese companions would wait to see what I had ordered, and then most or all of them would order the same. "Make it two—no, three—no, four." I asked about this. Yes, people would say; when I am in doubt, when I'm hovering, I order what other people are ordering, and when I'm with a guest I feel more comfortable following his lead. I thought: When there is not a foreigner to go first, how does anyone decide what to eat?

106

Figuring out how to do things is hard, but much harder still is figuring out what to do next. The profoundest malaise is that of the man who "does not know what to do"; he is at his most lost and dangerous. The same goes for a group. Every society must somehow set an agenda, but in a world of conflict this is not easy to do. The traditional solution has been to rely on a chieftain or leader to set the direction. This, however, too easily degenerated into authoritarianism, which was not only abusive but inept. No one in particular can ever know enough or have enough good sense to set the agenda for a society, or even to see his own mistakes. The great contribution of liberal social systems—democracy, capitalism, science—was to solve the agenda-setting problem. They are all public, competitive selection systems uniquely good at correcting old mistakes and making new ones. What to do next? There are always a million possibilities. Who will choose? The liberal innovation was to say: No one in particular will choose. Instead, everyone will compete for everyone else's support—support in the form of votes, money, and (in the case of science) belief. We all put our proposals on the table, and may the best one win. Of course a competitive selection system makes countless mistakes. But therein lies its genius: people will compete to correct them. Thus the system constantly regenerates its agenda and, over the longer term at least, regulates itself.

107

I began to see that living in Japan is like being perpetually on jury duty. The Japanese traditional values, with their hierarchic bent, could easily have legitimized the most brutal kind of dictatorship. To help neutralize that tendency, the Japanese emphasized unanimity as the source of legitimacy in social decision making: a decision isn't quite right until we all agree. Thus the renowned premium on "consensus," as the Japanese always call it. People have seen a peculiar Japaneseness in the Japanese aversion to nonconformism, but in fact there is similar intense pressure whenever everyone is supposed to agree before a decision can be declared—for instance, in the jury room.

108

That a unanimitarian society can work, and work well, is a fact to which Japan's success testifies. But certain accommodations must be made. You must avoid conflict, and where you cannot avoid it you must keep it personal (a few people not getting along) rather than making it public (a failure of unanimity and thus a social crisis). You must dismiss differentness as incidental. You must keep your disagreements tucked away in a drawer rather than airing them in public. I said earlier: Japan relies more heavily on conflict-avoidance than any society I have ever seen. That is because the Japanese put a higher premium on unanimity than any society I have ever seen. If you live in Japan, it is at least possible to believe—not that everyone actually does—that all differences of opinion, however numerous or profound, are merely incidental to the deeper reality of Japanese oneness, like waves on the surface of the deep sea. And to the extent that you are able to believe that way, you will feel enwombed.

109

The big drawback—and it is a very serious one—is that repression of conflict, however voluntary, makes agenda setting hard. When whatever the group is doing does not seem to be working, people have to edge warily toward a new consensus, eyeing each other all the while. First must come a general willingness to admit the old course's failure, which of course some people will hate to do; then the whole group must somehow find a new course that almost everyone is willing to follow. Often in such a case the group will just sit and molder until action is forced. On the other hand, a deadlock may be broken when everyone rushes precipitously after someone who darts off in a new direction. An American media-handler told me about a run-in with his Japanese counterparts. The gang of American journalists accompanying a grand dignitary in Japan was scheduled to be ushered past a secret defense installation. Looking is fine, the Japanese said, but absolutely no pictures. OK, said the Americans. All right then, said the Japanese, turn over all your cameras beforehand, and we'll keep them until the installation is out of sight. The Americans said, You've got to be kidding. They assured the Japanese that the journalists would be instructed to take no photos and would take none. Only after much haggling and with deep reluctance did the Japanese let the journalists hold on to their cameras. At last the reason emerged. In a group of Japanese reporters—so the authorities said—if only one person grabs a picture, the others, fearing to miss out, would instantly do the same. The situation would be out of control right away.

110

And of course people *will* disagree, and what then? Which course is legitimate? I happened to be in Japan in August of 1990, when the Iraqi dictator Saddam Hussein marched his army into Kuwait, provoking international outrage and a U.S.-led boycott of Iraqi and Kuwaiti oil. What was Japan going to do? The Foreign Ministry insisted that Japan join the boycott promptly, but the Ministry of International Trade and Industry and the Finance Ministry demurred, fearful of the effects on the economy. So the ministries were at odds, and the prime minister, lacking a consensus, dithered. Stalemate. Finally President Bush telephoned the prime minister, imploring him to do something, and the European Community joined the boycott, and under this pressure the two economic ministries buckled. A classic case, absolutely typical of the way Japanese decision making goes, and no less frustrating to the Japanese than to the foreigners. Later on in the same crisis, the Japanese leadership wanted to contribute medical teams to the international campaign against Saddam Hussein. But the constitution, very strictly interpreted, seemed to prohibit sending any military forces. The government was afraid it lacked a consensus to go with a less strict interpretation. The absurd result was that the government sent a handful of volunteer civilian doctors into a potential war zone, while ordering army doctors to stay safely at home. This had even the ministry people rolling their eyes. Around Tokyo, people were joking that anyone who wants a completely safe job need only join the Japanese army.

111

A people like the Japanese, who recoil from open conflict but who also will not abide stagnation, would seem to be trapped in a painful dilemma. If, as a society, they choose competitive liberal systems for making group decisions, they must live with, indeed encourage, public conflict. If they choose unanimitarianism, they risk agendaless drift. The remaining choice, authoritarianism, is worse than either of the other two. It suppresses conflict and makes quick decisions—but the decisions it makes are terrible and the conflicts it suppresses are essential. And so you would think that the Japanese are stuck—that they can have unanimity or an agenda, but not both. One of their great social achievements, I believe, was to discover an escape from this seemingly inescapable dilemma. I couldn't prove it, but I have a hypothesis: The Japanese would either have stagnated for lack of an agenda or turned to classic authoritarian rule in order to set one, but for a fortunate expedient. They learned that they could rely on outside competitive selection systems to set the agenda. Then they could grab the winner and run with it.

112

Call it parasitism if you want, or symbiosis if you prefer: but in any case call the strategy effective, for it has worked. Unanimity ("harmony," "consensus") was preserved within, steered and enabled by the guiding hand from outside.

Gaiatsu this is called: outside pressure. Actually, though, not just outside pressure (this is a point many people miss): also outside guidance and outside agenda setting. Is the Top Country building aircraft, making computer chips, planning ever-larger particle accelerators, wearing blue jeans, playing golf? Then that's what we'll do, only we'll do it better. To suggest that *gaiatsu* is uniquely a feature of Japan would be silly. The question is one of extent, which, in the case of Japan, is very large. One day, grousing about mindless Japanese imports of golf and violent movies, I complained to a Japanese friend that his countrymen had brought from outside everything that was evil except for NCAA football and the National Rifle Association. The very next day, the morning paper carried a story about the rising popularity of football among Japan's college athletes. Can the NRA be far behind?

113

A small political system—Mayor Daley's Chicago, for instance—can get away with single-party rule if the system is embedded within, and therefore constrained by, a larger one. And so for many years the Japanese City Hall has worked admirably, guided and constrained by foreign influence. Some sophisticates have maintained that the Japanese reliance on outsiders to set the agenda stems from a childlike dependence deep in the Japanese psyche. But no such psychobabble is called for. The Japanese have found that by letting outsiders make the toughest decisions, they could maintain peace and quiet within. Why bother with the open nastiness of oppositional politics when the Americans, or whoever, will do the job for you? And why should the ruling party engage in a divisive public debate over, say, Japan's role in the campaign against Iraq? Easier to let the Americans tell you what to do. Thus, in the postwar years, has Japan solved its agenda problem: by following the American political lead and chasing the American economic lead. The United States made the big international political decisions, and within the limits so demarcated little Japan could go about its business. That business—the whole Japanese policy in a nutshell—consisted mainly of two endeavors. First, distributing pork and protection to powerful domestic interests. Second, building the nation's base in industrial manufacturing. The so-called "special relationship" between America and Japan was a cozy deal for both sides. Japan gave America unwavering political loyalty, and in exchange America winked at Japan's equally unwavering economic opportunism. The Japanese got unanimity. The Americans got VCRs.

114

But what happens when Mayor Daley's Chicago is a super-power in most ways that count? One of the cliches that float around Tokyo is quite right: the United States is Japan's only effective opposition party. Thus the world is treated to the bizarre spectacle of Americans beating on the door for economic reforms that would mostly benefit Japanese shoppers; and thus taxi drivers ask meddling Americans to keep up the good work. By no means is it true that Japanese democracy is completely unresponsive. The ruling party stays in power by staying not too far behind popular opinion. The trouble is that response time is on the long side, and responses are on the minimal side, and City Hall is no substitute for the internal competitive balance-wheel of genuine oppositional politics. I believe that it is absurd for the world's second-greatest (and rapidly rising) power to rely on meddling from the outside to set its agenda and curb its excesses. Worse than absurd, indeed, it is dangerous. Meddling inevitably creates mutual resentment—and it is unsustainable anyway, because Japan is too big and too powerful now to have much to fear from the United States or anybody else. Sooner or later, and probably sooner, the Japanese public will realize its own strength. Soon not even the American government will be powerful enough to tell Japanese politicians what to do. What then? The post-*gaiatsu* era is upon us. It is here and no one is ready for it. I would much rather that the world's second great power have Tammany Hall's political system, as Japan does, than the Soviet Union's. But that leaves more room for worrying than I like.

115

I tried to be afraid of the economic system, but found that I could not be. Its secrets were altogether too mundane. There is no heart of darkness in the bureaucratic-corporate jungle of Japanese technofeudalism, no magic: mainly just reinstruction in what we thought we knew but never learned well enough. What has worked for Japan is what works everywhere: thrift, honesty, hard work, education, property rights, a willingness to sacrifice for tomorrow, and strong families that take good care of children. For the Japanese, it is true, there were some special circumstances: the horrible gift of a destroyed capital base, on which they could build afresh; a clear leader (the United States) whom they could focus on catching up to; the U.S.-Japan "special relationship," which made them secure. They also greatly accelerated the development process by turning it into a postwar national mission, impelled by the determination of each organization's members to be on the number-one team—for that's the ticket into the Ichi-ban Club. And they were impelled still further by the neurotic doctrines of Olympic Games (as opposed to neoclassical) economics, which say that high-glamour industrial manufacturing is like a sports contest, and that every trade has a winner and a loser (neoclassical says that every trade has two winners, or would not have happened); and so the Japanese were obsessed with high-glamour manufacturing, much as the East Germans were obsessed with their swimming team.

116

An old joke has a boy sitting in his front yard behind a sign: "Hamburgers, $1 Million Each." A passing grown-up helpfully tells him that he won't sell many hamburgers for a million dollars. "Yes," replies the boy serenely, "but I only have to sell one." Another old joke has a merchant selling all his wares below cost. "I lose money on every unit," he boasts. "But I make it up on volume." The jokes are absurd because obviously sales and profits are related. But if I were forced to choose my absurdity, I would choose the million-dollar hamburger. It pampers my sloth. I would certainly rather maximize profits than sales. My father, who was self-employed, used to say that money is applause. He could have said that sales are applause, but it would not have occurred to him to say that. Nor would it have occurred to me, until I encountered the Japanese obsession with market share. They will do anything to retain and increase market share. Sales are applause. To make sales is to build relationships (relationships are power) and to expand the circle within which one is an insider. To increase sales, then, is good for its own sake. One night at a sushi bar I met an American who worked in Tokyo for Salomon Brothers. What a Japanese company typically wants, he said, is no mystery. It wants to be "the biggest motherfucker out there." A nationalist crusade? No. More like a hankering for applause.

117

Often Americans become nervous and alarmed when confronted by the supercompetitive Japanese. We see their drive to win as implacable, relentless; we see their companies as market-eating machines that can neither be stopped nor diverted. What do they want, why don't they slow down? We forget that there was a time when American business executives also insisted on being the best, on being number one in the world in their line of work. No one could have persuaded us in those days that the American enterprising spirit was a threat to the rest of the world. And it wasn't. America's upstart industrial success added to prosperity not only in the United States but wherever people drove cars and used electric refrigerators. Perhaps Americans would be quicker to see how greatly we benefit from Japan's economic vibrance if the Japanese were as good at making new medicines and vaccines as they are at making new cars and computers. Research has estimated that the reliability of the average three-year-old car is improving consistently at a rate of five to six percent a year. We used to complain about planned obsolescence, about products built to fall apart; that's dead now, and we have Toyota and Sony to thank. We may say that Japanese companies merely usurped technologies and innovations that American companies would in due course have developed. But can anyone who remembers Detroit's cars in the 1970s really believe that? Our cars (the

American ones too) have improved, our electronic gadgets have improved, our lives have improved—only our egos have been hurt. If, however, the extraordinary Japanese contribution to global economic vitality today is greeted more with fear than with celebration, it is in no small measure the fault of the Japanese themselves. The intellectual virus of Olympic Games economics is catching. Commerce is the Olympics; market share measures national victory (or defeat); selling is strong and manly, buying is weak and decadent; if your team wins, then mine must have lost: by projecting these prescientific neurotic values, the Japanese paint themselves as an economic threat which in reality they are not.

Some people look at the Japanese economy and see a third way: something new, neither socialism nor capitalism, but instead successor to the former and challenge to the latter. I found this view to be nonsense. Japan has a cartelized economy like that of my American forefathers: in 1989, there were still 265 cartels officially blessed by the government, and today the largest six *keiretsu*, those thousand-tentacled networks of interlocked corporations (somewhat resembling the J.P. Morgan financial and industrial network in the early part of this century), account for fully fifteen percent of the economy's total assets and sales. I tend to think that Japan has succeeded more in spite of the cartels than because of them. Nokyo's agripolitical machine has hobbled farming productivity, hurting the Japanese who are shut in far more than the foreign farmers who are shut out. The small stores, for all their charm, are inefficient and expensive. Fixed commissions have ensured that the established securities houses will not be unduly inconvenienced by more efficient upstarts, and as a result have also ensured that Japanese investors will not be unduly able to make exchanges efficiently. Land policies make holding land cheap (property taxes are very low) but buying and selling land expensive (taxes on the proceeds are very high). This, characteristically, favors established stakeholders over newcomers, and as a side effect has led to rice fields remaining where high-rises ought to go, driving land prices ever further beyond the reach of the unlanded. (One day I asked a group of about twenty university students in Tokyo how many of them expected to be able to own a home. Half said yes, half said no—and all of those who said yes also said that they would inherit. Land frustration is becoming endemic among young Japanese. One professional man I met was so embittered over housing prices that he talked about emigrating.) Only recently has the tide begun to turn against the construction cartels, which routinely rig bids on public-works projects so as to spread the gravy and keep out upstarts. The practice raises construction costs and thus tends to depress the market for public-works improvements, so that the Japanese wind up with poorer roads—but the system does have the notable benefit of serving as "a major fundraising machine for the Liberal Democratic Party," as a newspaper succinctly put it. Add airline tickets, protection for weak banks—on and on.

119

If you want to know why Japanese policies have so strongly favored the interests of established big producers, you can look to two explanations. You'll hear one of them from the big producers and their friends in the government: that these policies were the key to the Japanese economic miracle, and that the wise company presidents and government officials understood as much and in their wisdom guided the process of development. The statement is sincere, and I suppose there might be some truth in it—though I know of little evidence to support it. True, by initially favoring the interests of big producers, for instance by using financial regulations to provide them with cheap capital, you can channel resources more quickly into building an industrial base, just as happened in late-nineteenth-century America. However, in postwar Japan, when everything had been flattened and there was nothing to buy, this would have happened anyway, with or without systematic favoritism toward big producers; and, of course, any economic benefits that such favoritism confers must be weighed against the costs of entrenched interests' free riding and cream skimming and market distorting. Nonetheless, the belief that what is good for big manufacturers and cartels is good for Japan remains deeply rooted.

One day, reading a museum guidebook, I saw the following explanation for the requirement that greengrocers of Edo-period Japan (two hundred years ago) "deal through the wholesale market of Edo [Tokyo] and buy from middlemen there. That's the rule for doing business in Edo. You have to operate in the established system of distribution. Everybody keeps this rule. That's why Edo could grow this big." See? Economies grow big because of benevolent monopoly middlemen. Thank you, mister monopolist.

120

On the other hand, you can go with the crass explanation, namely that the main reason for favoritism toward big producers has much less to do with economic efficiency than with political efficiency. Big producers are rich, concentrated, and dug in, whereas consumers and small savers are disorganized and diffuse. And so big producers tend to get their way. Q.E.D.

121

It is hard to argue with success, however. Never has an economy so much in need of perestroika, an economy so burdened with politically induced distortions, done so exceptionally well. That it has succeeded so brilliantly is a tribute to the hard work and flexibility of Japanese citizens, and also to the cartels' no-nonsense understanding that their franchise depends finally on their performance. A tribute, also, to an ingenious policy. Purely domestic industries in Japan—services, for instance, and retailing and construction—tend to be stagnant and inefficient in proportion as they are protected from newcomers. This is as one would expect. I leave my room in the morning and go down to the subway, where I find no machines to punch my ticket (actually, they are finally being phased in slowly) but a row of uniformed men punching each and every ticket by hand. (Think of it: in 1989, the Tokyo subway system sold more than 3 billion rides!) I go to the department store, where sales clerks are everywhere and attendants are running the automatic elevators. I stop at the grocery store and marvel at the full-time bag boy, a phenomenon not seen in my country since the late Mesozoic; I stop at the bank, and wonder what these swarms of employees could possibly all be doing; I think about my friend the bus attendant, paid to do the job of a DON'T WALK sign. I love the service in Japan. But I do not love that Japanese innovation, the five-dollar can of shaving cream. Why, then, is the Japanese economy so vigorous? How does it stay so sharply competitive? Highest priority went to the industries producing tradable goods, and these industries waged invigorating competition for foreign customers. After all, in the domestic sector a barrier to newcomers is a social relationship to be respected, but in the export sector it is a foreign-market challenge to be overcome. In large measure, stagnation was prevented by the good offices of that familiar strategy, reliance on external competitive systems to set the agenda.

122

I looked for and half found a soul-crushing center in the sprawl of the big-producer state. I often found a subordination of individuality to the ceaseless demands of the industrial machine, in which, it is true, the workers are expected to put the job well ahead of whatever comes second in their lives. The French observer André Siegfried has written a memorable description of this anti-individualist producer state. "What is absolutely new about this society which is accomplishing such marvels," he writes, "is that in all its many aspects—even including idealism and religion—it is working toward the single goal of production. . . . Hence a growing tendency to reduce all virtues to the primordial ideal of conformity. . . . The nation is not individualistic in mentality, and it therefore accepts this collectivism as part of itself; and the regime really suits it. The material advantages are so great, the security so perfect, and the enthusiasm of collective action in accomplishing stupendous tasks so overwhelming, that in an almost mystical abandon, other considerations are neither heeded nor missed.

"But can the individual possibly survive in such an atmosphere? In her enthusiasm to perfect her material success, has not America risked quenching the flame of individual liberty which Europe has always regarded as one of the chief treasures of civilization?"

123

Siegfried, as you see, was writing about America in 1927 (in *America Comes of Age*). I introduce him underhandedly in order to make a point. It is simply beyond doubt that for many years, although recently not quite as much, the Japanese suppressed individuality in themselves and each other. However, the crushing of individual spirit is easily and often exaggerated in accounts of Japan, just as it was exaggerated in Siegfried's account of America. On the one hand, it is true that the big companies and bureaucracies often can and do act as spiritual emptiers, turning human beings into company men. I remember one Japanese man telling me how his son, only a few weeks after graduating from college and entering one of the great companies, had been changed and flattened: he became less inquisitive, less lively, oddly and almost excessively polite. The boy was being corporatized. On the other hand, when I shopped in the stores or sat in the park on Sundays watching mom and dad (almost always *two* parents) out with the children, I found Japan too easygoing and "normal" and full of smiles—too much like my hometown—to support any notion that it is a country of robots or drones.

124

I saw my share of corporate marching morons, but I also
kept bumping into people like the architect who went into
business for himself because he wanted to see his own designs
built rather than a committee's, or the young women quitting
their jobs and staying single in order to go off to Europe
and America to study, or the freelance writers—more and
more of them—who prefer independence so that they can
write as they please. I found many workers (professionals and
white-collar people, mainly) who put the job first, just as my
father did for many years; but I also found many to whom the
job was just a job. I found many workers who had subsumed
their identity in the company's, but I also found them taking
evident pleasure in their company's effort to become *ichi-ban*,
number one. I found companies full of yes-men, but I also
found bars full of complainers. I found the corporate group-
calisthentics sessions, but I also found that many employees
simply ignored them. I found corporations making demands
for loyalty and unity of purpose that bordered on the totalitarian, but I also found companies that could be counted on
by their workers and so were worthy of loyalty: companies
that displayed nothing of the obscene decadence of American
managers like General Motors' Roger Smith, whose pension
was doubled to $1.1 million a year, even as the company un-
derperformed and its management took a tough line against
benefits increases for workers. In 1990, a recession year,

American corporate profits fell seven percent, but chief executives managed to pay themselves seven percent more. The chairman of UAL collected $18.3 million in pay and perks while the company's profits fell seventy-one percent (some employees' wages had been frozen for five years). This kind of behavior is unheard-of in Japan, incomprehensible. In American business, success means making as much money as you can before you get out; in Japanese business, success means being on the winning team. Guess which attitude turns out to work better in large-scale industrial manufacturing, which by its nature requires that hundreds and thousands of people work together?

125

In an office building colored violently blue so that everyone could see it, I entered the inner chamber of the Japanese industrial revolution. This was during the baking summer in Kumamoto prefecture, on the flatlands between the Kyushu coast and the mountains. I had seen two factories that day, one spanking new and one quite old, but both looking from the outside like corrugated-metal warehouses, promising little within but rolls of baling wire and stacks of crates. In fact the interiors were full of big computerized claws and robots and other machines used for building machines that would later build other machines. This was Hirata Industrial Machineries Company, whose employees numbered 1,100 and whose sales

ran to more than ¥20 billion a year. You will find many
robots at Hirata Machine but no MBAs, and indeed not many
college graduates: Hirata, like many Japanese companies,
prefers to grow its own, and hires something like seventy
percent of its workers from high school or trade school. They
build high-tech automated manufacturing systems, which in
turn make high-tech electronics equipment for consumers.

126

We founded the company in 1946, right after the war,
Yasunari Hirata told me. We spoke inside his office, somewhere within the disturbingly blue building. The Americans brought Jeeps with them after the war, he said, and
his father saw them and believed that conveyances, trans-
portation systems for industry, would be important. Father
and son—the son was young Yasunari—originally started out
by making pushcarts and baby carriages. The initial capital
investment was ¥3,000. Since the banks were unimpressed,
the Hiratas raised capital by saving money and wearing
old clothes. They started with old equipment that they re-
furbished. The engineers, including the founders, may not
have had much technical education, but they were willing to
learn and they loved doing new things, and whenever a new
machine arrived all the workers wanted to get their hands
on it. They tinkered with everything. Later on the company
graduated to making conveyor-belt systems. We learned as

we went along, he said, by trial and error and from books and traveling; we decided what to make and then figured out how to make it. Now we make industrial robots.

127

I see the company as an infinitely growing child, he said. I will die, but it continues to live, and my responsibility is to see to that. And I want to continue to build better and better robots. A better machine every year, that is what I want. You know: you don't have to have something to start something. —This he said with evident satisfaction.

128

I do not believe that the word "profit" would have passed his lips during our conversation if I had not brought it up. Profit? That was not his direct objective, he said, though at retirement he might liquidate some of what he had put into the company. Taxes are so high here you don't think much about profit, he said, chuckling. Earlier that day his business-planning manager had spoken of "bean counters" with contempt. At Hirata we never looked at profit-loss projections, he said: we looked at whether we could build a better machine. Whether this is literally true I would not want to say, but in any case what was most revealing was that they would talk this way. Yasunari Hirata, for his own part, was plainly not particularly interested in profits—not, I mean, in the sense of *taking* profits. He did not live lavishly and he seemed more concerned with immortality than with money.

129

Of course the story of Hirata Machine is the classic tale of Yankee ingenuity, transplanted to Kumamoto. It is a chapter from the book by Henry Ford and the others of that era. You remember that book. It is the one entitled "Build a better mousetrap and the world will beat a path to your door."

130

Yet the world bangs on the door with as much anger as eagerness. From an economic point of view, the Japanese economy must be counted among the miracles of our age, and ought to be regarded as an international treasure. It is a fount of innovation and instruction such as appears only once or twice in a century. But from the point of view of international politics, this same economy has been little short of a disaster. I met a number of Japanese who would have you believe that this is because the world does not like Asians in general and Japanese in particular, so that whites' achievements are welcomed, while the achievements of Japanese are resented. Perhaps that is a problem. Certainly it is a problem in some quarters. But it is not *the* problem, and those who look to racism for the source of Japan's international headaches, especially the headache with the United States, are kidding themselves.

131

The trouble has more to do with Japan's use of the outside world as a kind of garbage can for what economists call adjustment costs: that is, the costs of changing jobs, moving around, and breaking off relationships. A small country can protect its powerful stakeholders from troublesome adjustments without causing a great deal of fuss internationally. But the story is different for a large country, a country that is a great trading power. The combination of government protection and private clubs and cartels keeps many small farmers in business, but it also keeps foreign farmers out and so costs them money; and when the market at issue is very big and very rich instead of very small and very poor, the foreign farmers notice and are resentful. Same with the securities industry; same with the small-shops protection; same with the whole web of cozy relationships. Now, as a practical matter, it is not very likely that a de-cartelized Japanese farm sector or securities sector would make more than a small increment's difference in foreigners' living standards. International trade accounts for only a fraction of national income and Japan accounts for only a fraction of trade. In other words, there is not much reason to suppose that Japan's barriers to newcomers hurt anyone outside Japan very much. What upsets people is the principle, and therein lies the danger.

132

Though I know people who would disagree, personally I do not think that the tendency to dump adjustment costs on the outside world is caused by any special aversion to foreigners. (Nor is it uniquely Japanese. Everybody tries to do it.) I believe it simply has to do with the fact that foreigners do not vote in Japanese elections and are not tied into Japanese relationships. They lack both political pull and bonds of loyalty, and so are not cut in on the deals. Moreover, I do not think that the Japanese City Hall tries especially to thwart foreigners. Rather it tries to thwart newcomers. Unfortunately for the good of international relations, in Japan most foreigners are newcomers, and most Japanese are not. Now, in Japan, once you have established your personal ties and gotten in on your cozy deal, you are inside practically for good, whether you are foreign or not. Outsiders who are persistent and ingenious, and who are willing to pay the high initiation costs, do indeed get in, as for instance IBM and Coca-Cola (and Sony, once an upstart) have done. Then they enjoy fat profits, cozy relationships, and the other benefits of membership. Not long ago Pepsi began making rapid gains in the Japanese market, thanks to an especially popular TV ad—which was promptly dropped by Tokyo's major TV stations, under pressure from Pepsi's giant entrenched competitor. Pepsi understandably screeched and might, I suppose, have tried to list the issue among Japan's unfair trading practices, except that the entrenched competitor was Coca-Cola. The difference between them was not one of nationality but of position and thus power. Coca-Cola, however, is an exception. Inevitably most foreigners are still outside, and many of those have war stories to tell. One of my favorite is about the ingenuity, born of desperation, of an American meat-packing company and a Japanese beef importer who teamed up to sell U.S. beef. They got the usual newcomers' welcome. "We can't expand our sales of meat through the existing distribution," an executive of the beef-importing company was quoted as saying. "Beef sales are run by *keiretsu* producers"—that is, by groups of businesses tightly knit together by strong and often exclusive relationships. "They control the distribution of beef to retail stores." When last heard from, the partnership was trying to set up its own distribution channels—by selling frozen beef from vending machines. Not their first choice, this strategy.

133

So the outsiders get mad. Especially if they are Americans, who tend to get worked up about justice. The outsiders say, "Twenty and thirty and forty years ago, when you were flat on your backs, you were newcomers in America. Granted, life was not easy for you; but the easy-in, easy-out American system is paradise compared to what we encounter in Japan. Our economic hospitality put you on the map. And how is our hospitality returned? With cozy clubs and Byzantine relationships and 'Members Only' signs and lectures about 'not trying hard enough.' Well, screw you. We'll get even."

134

Hearing this, the insiders, the members of the Ichi-ban Club, are aghast. The plaintiffs have no case. Surely they misunderstand. The insiders say: "We worked out tails off to establish ourselves in America, whose markets were no pushover: we learned your language and studied your consumers and built distribution networks. We made a vast investment over many years. We played by your rules in your country, and we made the customer happy. And how is our effort repaid? You now demand to play by your rules in *our* country. Your automobile companies complain of 'closed' markets but do not manufacture righthand-drive cars. Is that our fault? Your executives don't learn our language; your companies come into a country where trust and personal ties are the coin of the realm and then pull out after losing money for a couple of years. How dare you blame us for that? No: you must not demand special treatment. You must pay the same dues that all newcomers pay in Japan, and if you do, you will enjoy the same benefits, and if you do not, you have no right to complain."

135

The argument belongs in an ethics textbook. Within its own context each side is wholly justified and has a strong claim to justice. And there exists no neutral ground from which to adjudicate. One must simply choose. A heartbreaker.

136

Worse, I fear: a bonebreaker. As the anger grows, the temptation becomes overwhelming for the nations of North America and Europe to say, "Two can play your game." Indeed, the Americans and Europeans, especially the Europeans, have been playing the game of protectionism for many years, and do rather well at it. All they need is an excuse to redouble their efforts. If they do so, then the result is either a trade war or recourse to a political solution in which governments meet to allocate markets. ("We'll buy this many Sonys if you'll buy that many Fords. You give us twenty percent of your computer-chip market in exchange for fifteen percent of our telecommunications market.") Either result is a disaster for Japan. Trade wars hurt most the countries that are most dependent on trade (read: Japan). And allocation of markets according to political clout, by its nature, favors the most politically powerful and hobbles the most economically competitive (read: Japan). This is why the Japanese are stupid and irresponsible to be anything other than the world's leading advocate of free trade, not merely following or complying but *leading*.

137

Moreover, Japan's practice of winking at cartels and ha-
rassing newcomers, however convenient for politicians
and stakeholders, hurts no one as much as the average
Japanese. As, indeed, many average Japanese are becoming
aware. Traveling abroad in increasing millions, they have
begun to see that coziness has its price: that by comparison with the United States or France they have two-thirds
as many miles of roadway for every car, that only about
two-thirds of their roads were paved by the late 1980s
(ninety percent in the United States, a hundred percent
in France and the United Kingdom), that apartment rents
were twice as high in Tokyo as in New York City, that
consumer prices were at least thirty percent higher than
in the United States, that Americans and Europeans took
for granted a number of household amenities—central
hot water, a toilet inside the apartment rather than down
the hall—which quite a few Japanese were getting along
without.

138

Therefore it is pretty clear in which direction the Japanese
should move: toward liberalization, voluntarily and fast. Not
because this is good for foreigners (although it is), but because
it is vital for Japan.

139

Yet almost always the Japanese still talk about liberalization and deregulation and the busting up of cozy insider deals as sops to angry Americans. "We'll do it," they say, "because that's what is required to mollify irate foreigners and avoid becoming a black sheep among nations." Thus they still tend to drag their feet rather than take the initiative. They tend to make changes only when the politicians can credibly tell the powerful insiders: We had no alternative. This is understandable, and indeed it is better to make needed changes slowly and reluctantly than not at all. But Japan is now a very big country, less and less dragable by Americans or anyone else. Dragging is requisite in no small measure because of the City Hall political system, which has stunted the forces that might have opposed and corrected from within the stranglehold of the clubs and special interests.

140

This is why I believe it to be very much in the interests of Japan and America alike to do what can be done to set going an internal competitive balance wheel—especially through political reforms, which might help only a little but, then again, might help a lot. The number of people who said that they welcomed American pressure suggests that a little more political competition might go a long way. Increased internal competition would tend to open Japan to newcomers, assuaging foreigners' feelings that they are being treated inhospitably. It would tend to reduce the distortions in the Japanese economy, which ripple outward to create tension and adjustment problems internationally. It would tend to ameliorate, in particular, the pro-producer bias, which causes so much fury among politically powerful foreign producers. Above all, increased internal competition would tend to establish an agenda-setting mechanism to replace foreign pressure, which each day becomes more impractical and dangerous.

141

There is not a great deal that Americans can do directly to reform the Japanese system, nor does international diplomatic etiquette permit them to try. However, at the very least Americans should avoid making blunders. The biggest blunder, and one that most Americans actually commit, is to see the goal as reducing the U.S. trade deficit. The U.S. balance of trade has little to do with Japanese economic practices and a great deal to do with macroeconomic forces in America—nor does it matter much anyway. Even people who try very hard have trouble finding any objective damage that trade deficits have caused to the American economy as a whole, and economic theory gives little reason to expect such damage. South Korea ran trade deficits chronically until 1986, and its industrial base was hardly falling apart. For the most part, America's industrial base also is not falling apart; and if it were falling apart, getting rid of the trade deficit would of itself no more solve the problem than shooting out the alarm would extinguish a fire. Unfortunately, however, in Olympic Games economics your trade balance is generally regarded as your score (minus you lose, plus you win). The tempting and dangerous trap is to seek commitments from the Japanese bureaucracy to manage away the trade deficit by playing macroeconomic games or, worse yet, by regulating imports and exports ("managed trade"). That kind of action would just reempower the administrative state, which blocks political and economic competition: precisely the wrong thing to do. Already the Japanese bureaucracy, like bureaucracies everywhere but less effectively opposed than most, tends to regulate everything that moves and keep secret everything that doesn't. (One day I read in the paper that the Construction Ministry had increased the permissible size of log cabins. Good news for Abe Lincoln.) At a time when market forces are slowly eroding Japanese bureaucratic power, the ministries would like nothing better than a mandate from the American government to regulate Japanese trade. The United States must avoid doing favors for Japanese bureaucracies and cartels. At every turn it must encourage measures that open the system to newcomers, and so to selection by competitive trial and error. Getting rid of the laws that protect small stores, or exposing the Nokyo agripolitical machine to foreign competition, is just the right sort of idea; demanding that the Construction Ministry dispense untold trillions of yen on public-works projects to jigger down the trade deficit, or demanding percentage shares of Japanese semiconductor markets, is the wrong sort of idea. The way to keep this straight is to set the important goal first: not reducing the trade deficit to some arbitrary number, but unwinding the coils of Japanese technofeudalism.

142

I want to add that the Japanese stand to gain in a particularly deep and important way from further movement in the direction of competitive liberalism. People on both sides of the Pacific always complain that the Japanese don't know what they want. The commentator and retired government official Naohiro Amaya likened Japan to a greyhound that has caught its rabbit (economic development) and no longer knows what to do. An American economist I know described Japan as a "goat's stomach," digesting whatever comes along until required by outside forces to change. The Japanese usually ascribe directionlessness to an absence of vision in the minds of the people. But most Americans have no grand vision beyond the shiny words "peace" and "freedom" and "democracy," and when they do they disagree: just like the Japanese. No: what is wanting is vision at the *system* level; and that is because Japan's unanimitarian system is at a loss to offer competing policy choices and so set an agenda. Countries do not know what they "want" until they hold competitive elections to instruct themselves. What Japan lacks is nothing more fundamental than a fully competitive mechanism for public self-revelation.

143

Yukichi Fukuzawa, the intellectual father of Japan's rush to modernization in the middle and late nineteenth century, complains in his autobiography that the bureaucracy of Japan is too strong and arrogant, the middle class too submissive, and the people too unreceptive to the West and its liberal ways. On all three counts Japan has made great strides, but I do not think that Fukuzawa's spirit is sleeping soundly quite yet.

144

The northern city of Sapporo erected a monument to the American educator William Smith Clark, inscribed with the advice that he shouted from his horse as he departed from the city in 1877: "Boys, be ambitious!" For many years Americans have been in the business of offering advice to the Japanese, not all of it as good as Clark's. I am self-conscious about having entered the advice business, because lately there has been an oversupply, and Americans have been talking when they would do better to listen. Where I have advised and criticized, it has been in the chin-stroking and, I fear, pretentious role of the benevolent American international citizen. ("Take two antimonopoly laws and call me in the morning.") In what follows, I venture into the kind of social system that is closest to my heart; and where I advise and criticize, I do so on the comfortable and unassailable grounds of prejudice and greed.

145

My prejudice lies in feeling that the most valuable and beautiful of all human products is not material but intellectual: the stock of tested statements that constitute our knowledge. Of course I am talking about science, but also about the social sciences, history, even criticism and journalism—the fields in which people search for truth about the world. My prejudice is that making knowledge is humanity's most important endeavor, and that to divert resources needlessly from this endeavor or to misuse them is a shameful waste. Similarly, my greed lies in my singleminded insistence that we never know enough or learn quickly enough. More, more, always more: when I see someone who could do more or better, I want him to get on with it.

146

For example, people sometimes (not often enough) take passing notice of the enormous amount of economic potential thrown away in the screwed-up markets of the third world and the Communist (or formerly Communist) countries. Yes. But it is more upsetting still to know that there are minds of extraordinary brilliance all over the world, thousands of them born every day, that are underdeveloped or underused. Only if they have the good fortune to gain access to the intellectual and educational institutions of the developed free countries are they ever likely to be nurtured and heard from. One could say much the same of America's inner cities. With human beings the trick is not to produce brilliance but to use it.

147

My own impression of Japan is this. The intellectual raw material is top-notch, as good as any in the world. Again and again I met people with remarkable minds. Yet here is a country with the world's most vibrant economy, with a well-educated citizenry singularly devoted to making the country better, with a population fully half the size of America's and more than half again the size of Germany's, yet with only five Nobel prizes in science to its name—one thirtieth America's share, one twelfth Germany's, and exactly as many as Belgium's. Yes, Nobel prizes are an inexact measure of nothing in particular; but my own experience in Japan confirmed the story that the Nobels seem to tell—a story of wasted intellectual resources. Japan has all that is necessary to make a magnificent contribution to the world's stock of knowledge, but it is failing to do so.

148

The intellectual raw material being as good as it is, the level of education and of prosperity being so high, one must look to the social system to see why mediocrity has triumphed where brilliance should be. In universities and schools, in editorial offices and newsrooms, in government offices, I talked with people who were part of the knowledge industry. Patterns began to emerge.

149

We are all looking for each other's mistakes. Science, like Japan, has been wildly overmystified. When you cut through to fundamentals, the whole liberal intellectual system, from the hard sciences to history and even to journalism, is really little more than an endless self-organizing hunt for error. We develop ideas and then, like stage mothers, shove them out into public view, knowing that if we are found right we can become famous and that if we are found wrong we can try again; then countless others look for holes, shortcomings, weaknesses, poking and prodding, knowing that whoever finds a big mistake can become famous; in reaction the ideas are refined, reformulated, resubjected to public criticism; and what is left standing on any given day is our knowledge. In this way, knowledge moves forward. Why is it a "liberal" system, as democracy and capitalism are? Because it is a public competitive-selection system that fixes rules rather than outcomes or special authorities. Everyone is entitled to check anyone, and no one is immune to being checked just because of who he or she happens to be. We rely on no one in particular to sort the true from the false and the fruitful from the frivolous.

150

"Particularly at school," a prominent Japanese journalist told me one day, explaining why Japanese baseball is so dull, "we are trained not to make a mistake, even if this means we achieve nothing spectacular." At retirement, he said, Japanese tend to express satisfaction not by speaking of their accomplishments but by saying that they made no big mistakes. One often hears variations on this theme— the Japanese hate to make mistakes—and on the whole I found it to be true. The exception is where everybody makes the same mistake together, in which case it is not a mistake. A physicist told me that his career was set back five years by a single putative (he disagrees) mistake. Junichi Nishizawa, one of Japan's best-known scientists, told me, no doubt a bit hyperbolically, that if you make a mistake in your research "you never get another chance," or in a liberal university maybe just one other chance—in any case, not enough. Now, aversion to error makes people careful, and there is nothing wrong with that. Especially not in industrial manufacturing, where the idea is to make large numbers of things perfectly, and where the Japanese genius for quality control has given the rest of us a humbling reminder of the importance of getting it right the first time. But aversion to error can also suffocate knowledge, if the conditions are not just so.

151

Conditions? Is something wrong? Missing? I met many Japanese who thought so. The writer and critic Shuichi Kato told me: in Japan disagreement is regarded as an unfortunate accident, an embarrassment to be papered over. Book reviewers told me that, in general, if they didn't like a book they simply did not review it, or returned it to the editor to be reviewed by someone who did like it. Book reviews, people complained, are typically valentines or summaries, on the theory that if you can't say something nice you shouldn't say anything at all. To dislike a book publicly and explain why, they said, was uncommon. Why use up space on a book you can't recommend? (And why, the more cynical observers added, spoil your connections with another writer, who may soon be reviewing your own book?) "An open debate," a Tokyo University economist remarked to me one night over dinner, "is nearly impossible in this country."

152

I often heard comments of that sort. Yet nowhere in Japan is there even a hint of the kind of centralized intellectual authoritarianism that Plato advocated and that since his time has become so familiar in the West, thanks to the big churches and the totalitarian states. There is no propaganda, no state manifesto in Japan. The Japanese are nature's own empiricists, and it would no more occur to them to kill for a theory than to die for one. As a matter of fact, where institutional regulations are concerned, Japanese academics are more free than their American counterparts: they receive tenure from the moment they are hired, and thenceforward are free to say or write anything they want. Moreover, although some people have said that Japan is a place where nosy neighbors and high-handed bosses and government ministries effectively stamp out dissent, I found this to be unsupportable. In Japan, dissenters and minorities are not crushed, they are ignored or marginalized. If you feel like saying something different, and quite a few people do, you can say it with every expectation of personal safety and financial security, though also with little expectation of changing anything. There is an important exception: violent right-wing extremists have succeeded in making people watch what they say about the emperor's person or throne. In December 1988, Hitoshi Motoshima, the mayor of Nagasaki, dared to say publicly that the emperor bore some responsibility for the war. It was an act of great courage, and one for which he paid: he was later wounded in an assassination attempt. But this is the exception. On the whole, people speak out vocally and critically all the time. But something is amiss.

153

Science in particular and liberal inquiry in general consist of an infinite variety of activities, but one rule is necessary as a minimum. We say: it is one thing to attack someone's theory, quite another to attack his person. "Of course I respect Professor Nosebinder, but his theory is absurd for the following six reasons." Actually, the distinction between proposition and proponent is an artifice, since propositions do not exist by themselves; science is littered with theoretical debates that broke down into personality contests and even feuds. But the important thing is that it is not respectable for this to happen, and if you take criticism of your ideas as a personal insult, people are likely to say, "Oh, grow up." This is the principle, the social convention, that allows us to conduct public debate without severing personal ties: we kill our hypotheses, not each other.

154

In Japan, this convention exists but stands like a plant stuck upright in thin topsoil and only barely rooted. Masao Maruyama, the famous intellectual historian, pointed out to me one day that the very concept of "opposition," as distinct from "enmity" or "antagonism," did not exist in Japan until the last century; when Yukichi Fukuzawa returned from the West in the mid-1800s, he had to invent a word (*hantai*) for "opposition" in this nonpersonal sense. Nor was there a word for "speech" in the sense of an address to one's peers, as distinct from preaching or issuing decrees or other forms of address from a higher-up to lower-downs. Fukuzawa also had to invent words for "support" or "agree," and for "debate" or "discussion" in the sense of open exchange and confrontation of ideas—so unfamiliar was the notion of social intercourse between ideas, as it were, rather than between particular persons. Even today, criticism tends to be taken personally and even viewed as an act of antagonism. This attitude is common enough everywhere, but in Japan the weight of social convention is not against it.

155

In a place where unanimity is the legitimizer of social decisions and where personal ties are relied upon to resolve conflict and get things done, actions that cause enmity and break social ties are dangerous to everyone. They are a threat to the peace. And so criticism is a risky business. Not, however, because someone sends the KGB after you. Rather because there is a general awareness that, under the circumstances, open criticism of somebody's idea is socially irresponsible. It tears the web. Thus public criticism and social responsibility are pitted against each other—whereas the liberal tradition makes them allies. I suspect that this is why Japanese train themselves to be so averse to error: the best way to obviate the need for divisive public criticism is not to be wrong in the first place. Avoiding mistakes is the socially responsible thing to do.

156

I watched one night as one of Japan's most prominent political scientists, a dignified man in his sixties, turned as ebullient as a schoolboy. He was explaining how much he enjoyed academic meetings abroad, and to show what he meant he waved his hand eagerly and exclaimed like a boy in class, "I disagree, I disagree!" He said: In academic meetings in Japan you're supposed to listen expressionlessly; to raise a hand and object would be seen as odd, impolite, inappropriate. His work in English was criticized by foreign scholars, but his work in Japanese was not criticized by Japanese scholars. The best policy toward ideas you disagree with, he said, is one of benign neglect. 'The best policy here is to be mute," he said. "Year after year you get accustomed—you get trained."

157

I said: But surely, *sensei*, a man of your eminence is at liberty to criticize when he pleases? No, he replied, on the contrary;

the eminent have a special responsibility to restrain themselves if they cannot agree. The saying goes that when the wind blows, the tallest stalk of wheat must bow with the others. He no longer bothers going to academic meetings in Japan. To test ideas, he relies instead on more frank private exchanges with other scholars and thinkers— people who know and trust each other. I said: An intellectual black market, so to speak? More like a gray market, he replied.

158

I cannot say it too often: this is not political repression or fundamentalist brainwashing. It is not the Soviet Union before glasnost, nor is it Iran under the rule of the totalitarian priesthood. It is not remotely like that. The essence of totalitarianism, from the Inquisition to the present, is the network of informers, the midnight arrest, the secret trial in which the accused is charged with believing incorrectly. You will not find any of that in Japan. Indeed, scarcely a day passes in Tokyo when you are not annoyed by political activists blaring high-decibel foolishness from sound trucks.

159

Why, then, do I harp on criticism this way? Because people have missed the point about knowledge-making in Japan. Especially the Japanese have missed it. We aren't innovative, they complain, not creative. Typical was an editorial headlined "Wanted: Secrets of Creativity." No, no, no. The root of the problem is not creativity. In Japan, as any visitor to the high-tech wonderland of the electronics stores will testify, there is plenty of creativity. It is practically running in the streets, *if* the creativity is salable and so there are incentives not to waste it. No: the crucial shortage is of curiosity and checking. Curiosity because to be curious is to look for mistakes, your own and other people's. Where curiosity is lacking, creativity turns imitative. And checking is more important still, because without it, all the creativity in the world is like so much water trickling away between the fingers. Having new ideas is easy. You can do it three times a day before breakfast. But most of your new ideas will be bad. The hard part is to sort the grains of gold from the mountains of sand. The liberal scientific system has convincingly demonstrated that the most efficient way to do the sorting is to link as many people as possible in a network of intellectual exchange, and then to expose everybody's ideas to critical examination from everybody else. The success of this method has been extraordinary.

160

In Japan, however, the preference for benign neglect means that new ideas often just lie there on the table. So do the old ideas, until people grow tired of them. Not always, but too often. The Tokyo University economics department is really two departments. One is made up of younger faculty members trained abroad in neoclassical economics and taking part in the international academic discussion, though rarely in the lead of it. The other is made up of Marxists in the grand old tradition, going through their paces as in days of yore before Communism collapsed, bringing up young scholars to replace them, and just hanging on, unchecked and unchecking. Whenever I gave a talk in Japan, it would just sit there, regarded by the audience as a museum piece. Rarely was I questioned directly. That would be rude.

161

No drive through West Texas, not even a *New York Times* editorial, could be as dull as an academic meeting I attended in Japan. Actually it was a discussion of some of the implications of nuclear power, and an intelligent and thorough discussion at that. But too thorough and, come to think of it, not much of a discussion. The presenter just presented, reciting facts in excruciating detail, without a hint of theory. This, I was later told, was not unusual. Empiricism—the retreat to facts, to what can be commonly agreed upon—is science's main ploy for keeping the peace when people are at odds over theory and interpretation. True everywhere. But Japanese academic work, I was told, and also articles in magazines and the like tend to be either numbingly empirical or sweepingly polemical. I can't read Japanese, but the articles I saw in translation tended to back up the observation. Not surprisingly. Empiricism occasions little conflict and so is socially safe. By the same token, a polemic, the stringing together of flat assertions, offers few checkable facts or refutable theories. You just take it or leave it, depending on your sympathies. Both extremes, in that respect, differ from checkable theory, which goes out begging for a fight.

162

In Japan, it emerged, the tendency in testing propositions is to rely on the gut test and the grapevine test. In the gut test, you digest a new idea and see how it sits. You observe how it sits with others. Over time, the sum of private ruminations produces some ideas that stick around and others that do not. The gut test works in partnership with the grapevine test. In the grapevine test, you use backroom banter and private criticism to check ideas: gossip, sharing of confidences, hallway discussions ("What did you think of so-and-so's new book?"). These methods are heavily used everywhere. But in and of themselves they are inefficient and clumsy, taking forever to put the right ideas and checkers together, when they manage to do so at all. They are no substitute for far-flung public debate. Being private, very local, and purely reactive, the gut and grapevine tests are dreadfully cumbersome for sorting out the ideas that are most worth pursuing—cumbersome, that is to say, for setting the agenda.

163

So who sorts the winners from the losers? Who else?—foreigners. *Gaiatsu.* The outside competitive-selection system sets the research agenda, and then the Japanese go to work on it.

164

A physicist complains that the government bureaucrats who approve the research budgets at the national universities are always looking for the sure thing. As a result, preference goes to elaborated versions of experiments already successful abroad, rather than to virgin explorations. (This kind of double-checking is important, but the Japanese could be doing much more.) A prominent statistician says that the academic and governmental bureaucrats who underwrite research usually wait until an idea has become fashionable abroad before they consider it "certified" as worthy of pursuit in Japan—even if the idea originated in Japan. He recites a list of Japanese mathematicians and statisticians whose pathbreaking work was ignored until foreigners discovered it or independently rediscovered it. Junichi Nishizawa, renowned for his work in electrical engineering, recites similar cases with evident disgust. In the case of a recent invention of his own, he says, the "sad fact" is that he must arrange to have the device used in the United States before he can convince his own countrymen of its value. "Japanese have low evaluation for Japanese results," he says, "but they have a very high evaluation of foreign work." He himself publishes almost exclusively in foreign journals: "Japanese cannot evaluate my ideas." A famous political scientist refers to Japanese as "importers and distributors" of foreign ideas—franchisees, as it were. Whole debates are picked up and imported to Japan, but not the critical mechanism that generates the *next* debate. So he said. So said others. What surprised me the most was hearing from some of the country's leading scholars that, even in the field of Japanese studies, domestic scholars do top-notch empirical work, but the theoretical agenda is mainly set by foreigners.

165

Intellectual *gaiatsu* has few untoward international side effects. It causes no trade friction and incites no diplomatic incidents. It merely—"merely"—keeps the Japanese intellectual establishment one step or two steps behind, always inside the frontiers of knowledge rather than extending them.

166

Not surprising, then, that the Japanese literary system is relatively good at generating output but relatively bad at sorting it. The Japanese may be the world's most literate public, and the demand for books and articles is voracious. There are almost 4,000 magazines, the majority of them weeklies; the sales of magazines increased by almost sixty percent between 1980 and 1989. Moreover, open any of the major highbrow magazines and you will find a bewildering number of articles—in the monthlies, forty and fifty in each issue. Most of the editors I talked to believe that this is too many, but no one wants to be the first to cut back and risk losing readers to the competition. As for books, in 1989 alone 38,000 new ones went into print. (America, with twice the population, publishes about 50,000 titles a year.) In America, book writing is the great authorial challenge, a heroic trek up literary Everest, even though most books are hardly read and soon disappear. We are all Michelangelos when we are writing our books. The Japanese have spared themselves the romantic folly of seeing every book as a monument for the ages; they view a book as something to be knocked off so that one may get started on the next book. It is common for people to write a book or two, or three, a year. One critic I know has published at least a hundred. Taichi Sakaiya, in the decade and a half since he first took up writing, published ten novels and nineteen works of nonfiction; by Japanese standards he is not especially prolific. Another writer I met has written articles by the pound and twenty books in the last fifteen years, but a third of those, he freely owns, are not very good. Lower average quality is inevitable when fees are low. People often write books by dictating them into tape recorders.

167

Japan occupies the high-volume end of the literary demand curve. Books are inexpensive, and they are sleek and elegant by comparison with their overweight, sloppily made American counterparts. For authors, however, the pay is low unless you are one of the fortunate stars whose name generates large sales. Magazine fees are also low by comparison with fees in the United States. To keep themselves clothed and fed, writers write and write, and write and write and write. They need the money and the editors need the copy. Editors shovel out the assignments in order to maintain secure connections with their writers, who otherwise might drift into the orbit of some other magazine; writers rarely turn down assignments, because it is important to maintain secure connections with the editors, who otherwise might hire other writers. And so articles pour forth in staggering profusion, generated by editors and writers locked in the embrace of what Sakaiya calls a "culture of quantity." A young writer I know cranks out ten monthly columns for various magazines, on subjects from new books to hot rods to trends in Tokyo—this output in addition to the many irregular articles and, of course, the books. He enjoys the exposure and makes good money, but he has no time for friends and worries about keeping up the pace as he gets older, especially since he regards himself as a writer rather than a showman and does not want to go on TV. His integrity will cost him, because the trick is to get on

TV so as to break into the speech-making market. Speaking, unlike writing, is lucrative—especially speaking to corporate audiences. You can make a lot of money, Shuichi Kato once told me with contempt, if you are willing to be an intellectual geisha.

168

The upshot is that the Japanese literary market is extraordinarily, indeed enviably, open and vital where sheer rambunctious quantity is concerned. On the other hand, people who read both languages well tell me that the Japanese bookshelves are more heavily stocked with dross than even the American ones. In the United States it is hard to get published but easy to get checked; in Japan it is easy to get published but hard to get checked. The problem in Japan is not a lack of raw creativity, it is checking—setting ideas in conflict to sort the worthy from the foolish.

169

Much is being lost. In their single-minded determination to catch up with the West technologically and economically, the Japanese have built their society to feed and support industrial manufacturing. That is to be expected in a developing country (to a degree it happened in the United States during the last century), but in Japan it has gone too far for too long. The best minds are lured by prestige into manufacturing companies and into the bureaucracy that serves manufacturing companies; once there, the fine minds lose their fizz and go flat. Industrial manufacturing is served well, yes. But that is not the most important thing to serve. The universities ought to be bubbling today but are not; they were founded as organs of the national developmental effort a hundred years ago and have not outgrown their original stunted mission. The first article of the Imperial University ordinance of 1886 reads: "The purpose of the imperial university shall be to provide instruction in the arts and sciences and to inquire into the mysteries of learning in accordance with the needs of the state." Michio Nagai, a former minister of education, has written that the 1886 ordinance, which speaks of knowledge as a servant of the state, embodies a central confusion that cripples Japanese universities to this day. "It is not an exaggeration to say that education designed to develop men who love learning and think for themselves has already been abandoned," he writes. "Universities have come to be regarded as nothing more than training institutes for salaried men, doctors, engineers, and persons in other practical professions." Many of the major companies prefer new recruits whose minds are clean slates rather than full of college learning, and so training in skeptical inquiry is less attractive than it ought to be. As for think-tanks, Japan is full of them, but by and large they focus on economics and economic development ("in accordance with the needs of the state"). The work they do is solid and professional, but their agenda is narrowed by the narrow interests of the corporations and government bureaucracies that provide the bulk of their commissions and research fees. Economics is important, but there is more to life than capital allocation and regional growth forecasting. What about the cycles of the earth, the theory of political struggle, the history of man, the stars?

170

In time will Japan take its rightful place as one of the world's great intellectual fountainheads? Two Japans, again. Older people were gloomy: the situation, they tended to say, is changing only very slowly, and in many ways not for the better. "It is getting worse," Masao Maruyama said. "What is important for us is conclusions, not the process that makes the conclusions." Younger people were optimistic. A fresh generation, often trained in American and European graduate schools and less averse than their elders to errors and criticism, is moving up, they said; gradually the society is diversifying, the quality of the theoretical scholarship improving. And me? I lean, I suppose, toward the optimists. But for Japan to establish a critical culture, and so be able to bring the full power of her intellectual resources to bear on today's problems, will take at least a generation, probably two or three. In the meantime we will have lost a good thirty or fifty years. An immense loss this is, an irretrievable loss.

171

At the base of the intellectual system, and thus at the bottom
of the curiosity shortage, are the schools. One day I saw their
two faces back to back, like the faces of Janus, at a junior high
school in Oita prefecture. One cannot help being impressed
by the schools in Japan, for better and worse. Given the usual
preconceptions about Japan's discipline and conformism, the
elementary schools come as a surprise: very much like their
American counterparts in the early grades, full of life and
noise, and also less neurotically straitened. When I was in
kindergarten the teacher used to make us form lines "straight
as a pencil" whenever we left the classroom. Straight lines set
the tone for elementary school every year—constant supervi-
sion, incessant demands for quiet and order. In the Japanese
elementary schools the children travel in small mobs, and
during lunch break they jabber and zoom around on the
teacher's swivel chair like so many little bandits, while the
teacher—a woman, reliably professional and competent—
seems not to notice. "Seems" is the operative word, for the
children are being trained in the cardinal rule of Japanese
social life: you can do whatever you like, as long as you
don't test the limits. (American elementary schools, with
their pencil-straight lines always drawing clear boundaries
between what you can and cannot do, teach the cardinal rule
of American social life: test the limits, and then do as much as
you can get away with.) Sure enough, the Japanese children

generally don't test the limits; after the lunch break, classes are orderly and crisp. In Niigata, I watched third-graders in math class adding fractions (2/3 + 3/5—in third grade!) and chattering quietly and raising hands and shouting "chigaimasu!"—wrong!—at wrong answers and generally having a good time. There was something of this atmosphere, too, in the physics lab I watched at the junior high school in Oita: groups of students were clustered around lab tables, talking excitedly as they dipped weights into graduated cylinders, while the teacher casually roamed the room. Yet in the neighboring room I saw the stony face of the other Japan. "The nail that sticks up gets hammered down," says the proverb; and junior high school, grades seven through nine, is where the hammer begins its descent. Here, in biology class, were the uniformed students arrayed in rows, poring over notes and diagrams that they were meticulously copying from the blackboard while the teacher, hardly noticing the students, droned through his lecture. Back to back these two classrooms, as though in contest.

172

By high school the contest is settled. The teacher talks, the students silently take copious notes for later memorization, and the test—the inevitable almighty test in this country of tests—renders unassailable judgment. So it is, at least, for students who want to go to college. Toward the end of high school they starve themselves of sleep (five hours a night) and cut out clubs and sports in order to cram for the university entrance exams. Many of them go to school after school, known as *juku* (often rendered as "cram school"). Entry to all the best ministries, universities, high schools, junior high schools, and even *juku* is by test, and for every test there is a *juku*. A man I know sends his ten-year-old daughter to *juku* for nine hours a week, to ready her for the junior-high entrance exams. That is not necessarily the limit. At one prestigious *juku* the principal told me that a third of his students— all of whom were in the elementary grades—attended yet another *juku* in addition to their six hours a week at his own. Such students might typically get home at eight o'clock, eat dinner, and then do homework for two or three hours. Faced with such drivenness one doesn't quite know whether to be admiring or horrified.

173

Actually, the sweatshop overtones of "cram school" are misleading. Because they are private and must compete for students, *juku* offer some of the best and liveliest instruction in Japan. But they have one mission only: to teach the test. That is all. In Oita, where there were no good private *juku*, the high-school teachers themselves taught classes after class, trying to cram their students into the best colleges. In one such class I saw the teacher grill students on fine points of classical Japanese (it's on the test); the students muttered answers barely audibly from their seats, and if they made a mistake they sat on the floor until they could redeem themselves with a right answer. Another teacher was going over a practice exam in geography (there are lots and lots of practice exams; Japanese college-bound students become very skillful at test taking). Students had to identify unnamed American cities from the latitudes and longitudes and climates and so on. Why anyone would need to memorize latitudes and longitudes was beyond me—but I had missed the point, for this was an exercise in diligence. Japanese secondary education, and to a large degree even college education, is not about learning to ask the right questions. It is about learning to give the right answer, of which there is exactly one: the one on the test.

174

How grim it all sounds, spelled out this way on paper. But what you see is not grim at all. High spirits and smiles abound in the high schools. How is that possible? Team spirit, partly, and the satisfaction that goes with doing well what is expected of you, and also the knowledge that once you're admitted to college you can take a four-year vacation if you want to. And something else: practically everybody supports the exam system in principle, even the people who think it has got out of hand in practice. College admissions are a high-stakes game, since the status of the college you get into is a key determinant of whether you can get one of the top jobs and so join the Ichi-ban Club. The top ministry jobs are filled almost entirely from Tokyo University, for instance. And so the way Tokyo University and other colleges admit their students becomes a pressing social question, and fairness is a paramount concern. People feel that it would be unfair to make such an important determination even slightly arbitrarily (read: subjectively), and so they set up a test that anybody can take and that scores everybody on the same scale, down to a fraction. Never mind that the test measures the ability to memorize trivia; it is fair. Essay answers and letters of recommendation need subjective readers, and subjectivity engenders conflict; the objective tests avoid it; the choice is obvious.

175

The crushing of curiosity is, I think, a side effect, not a goal. But in any case it is the result. In all the classrooms I visited in Japan, from kindergarten to university, I never once saw a student ask a question. High-school students told me they didn't want to stick out or be laughed at. Teachers believe, rightly, that minutes spent on questions are minutes diverted from preparation for the exams. By the time students reach college, a professor who wants questions—and most don't, preferring to drone mechanically from their notes—has to drag them out of some unfortunate and embarrassed student. It's not worth the trouble it causes. I asked whether students see professors after class. Yes, the professors answered, but almost always for instructions rather than to satisfy curiosity. In small seminars at top universities you can get a discussion going if you prime the pump enough, especially if there are a few "returnees" from American or European schools to crack the placid surface. But the prevailing norm is the room full of students, sitting passively like so many empty vessels, waiting and expecting to be filled. They copy, or simply sleep, while the professor reads from his notes. It is horrendously dull, dull enough to make one's knees and back ache, so dull that students as often as not skip class and copy a friend's notes later. I visited one class in which a professor was droning to eighteen students. But the room was large, so I asked how many were enrolled. Two hundred, came the answer. I would have stayed home too: the purpose of such classes is to acclimate people to boredom, I suppose for the good of industrial manufacturing. In the United States we say that elementary schools teach socialization, high schools teach independence (and, these days, not much else), and universities teach students to question what has gone before and so in that sense *de*socialize. In the Japanese schools, socialization goes on right through college. The cost to human knowledge is, I believe, very high.

176

At first I saw the Education Ministry, known in Japan as the Mombusho, as the reptilian presence at the center of the system, hissing and darting at all attempts to make reforms. The Mombusho sets the basic curriculum, chooses the approved textbooks, pays the largest share of the bills, finances and regulates the public universities, charters and subsidizes and regulates even the private universities. It is all but inescapable in Japanese education. But I was wrong. The Mombusho people are nothing worse than well-intentioned bureaucrats engaged in a misguided project—namely, seeing that schools in Japan are all basically alike—and they do this largely because the public insists on equality, and gets far more of it than Americans do. (The Japanese schools produce a high average and relatively few performers who are either very strong or very weak.) "In order to compete in society," one former Education Ministry official told me, "all students should be given an equal competitive basis; that is our phi-losophy." You may think the philosophy misguided, but most Japanese support it. Interestingly, in recent years it has been none other than the Mombusho that has advocated change, albeit only very gradual change. But reform is impeded by the very existence of a powerful, centralized education bureau-cracy with a hankering for uniformity (what everybody does can't be wrong). How, for instance, do you foster creativity from the Mombusho headquarters in Tokyo? You put it in the curriculum, of course: "Life Environment Studies." People are used to taking instructions from the center, even when the center would rather they didn't. When the Mombusho created a weekly elective hour that schools were supposed to use creatively, the schools, at a loss, besieged the ministry until at last it had to issue creativity guidelines. When the ministry does try to make reforms, it comes up against all the well-intentioned others: test-obsessed parents, entrenched professors and teachers, conservative local school boards, and complacent politicians, all of whom have the power to block or stall reforms, and all of whom use it. And, understandably, no one wants to upset too radically a system that produces so few discipline problems and so many students who can handle differential calculus. In those respects, the Japanese schools are the envy of the world. Japanese third-graders add fractions and don't complain about it; third-graders in New York City are regarded as working at grade level if they can handle the following subtraction: "There were 12 birds in the tree. Then 9 flew away. How many birds were left?" According to the surveys, Americans think that children receive a better education in Japan than in America. Ironically but perhaps not so very surprisingly, Japanese think otherwise; polls show that most of them are dissatisfied with the schools. But predictably people are divided over which way to go with the education system and how to get there. There's no *gaiatsu*, so who's to decide?

177

I was just a sociological tourist in Japan. I took notes and drew maps, looking about me as only the outsider can do. I did not find The System, a capitalized entity weaving its web around the hapless common man. I found, in the end, just systems. There was no dark secret. The Japanese are precisely as mysterious and unique as my aunt in Hackensack. I came to Japan wanting to know how I ought to feel about the place. I left knowing only how not to feel. Frightened: that is how not to feel.

178

Worried, yes, to the extent that Japan is a great power whose social institutions are consistently, perhaps fundamentally, hobbled by the trouble they have setting an agenda. A powerful nation which is too big to push around but which often cannot push itself: that is Japan. "I am very much ashamed to say this," Masao Maruyama said to me one night: "Japan can change only under outside pressure—ever since Perry." I am not very worried, however. These things tend to work themselves out, as long as nobody panics. One day, in exasperation at the latest article about the U.S.-Japan crisis and the threat to the world order, I thought: "I wish people would stop hyperventilating about Japan."

179

One thing, though, I do believe, especially about the high schools, the treatment of women, and the political system's smoke-filled rooms. The Japanese people deserve better social institutions than the ones they have.

180

Foreigners sometimes say that the Japanese are to be feared because they lack principles. Indeed, the Japanese say it too. We have no principles: that is our problem. So I was told by Japanese more than a few times. Like other clichés, this one is exaggerated but true enough to be worth something. I had expected to be upset by the vacancy of ideology—I of all people, since ideas and principles are my obsessions. In the end, though, I was not upset. If you don't proclaim principles, you won't be a hypocrite. Personally, I would rather have the principles and take the hypocrisy, but it is undeniably refreshing to be in a place as unhypocritical as Japan. Besides, for most of the past two thousand years, the majority of principles have been bad. (Someone—who?—once said that a principle is not fully worthy of the name until it has killed somebody.) I found it refreshing that the Japanese don't much bother their heads with hypocritical twaddle about romantic love. They are as unideological about love as about most other matters. When I asked a young Japanese friend of mine when she and her husband fell in love, she replied that they didn't, though, she said, "We had our moments." They married because they saw that they would make a compatible social team. The Japanese see marriage as an investment, not as consumption, and they make it pay off rather than throwing it out when it gets old. That is one reason why children—another social investment—are never left to chance in Japan, whereas in America half of the children will experience a family breakup before their sixteenth birthday, a fourth live with only one parent, and a fifth live in poverty.

181

Although the country monopolized my fascination, I was finally unable either to love it or to fear it. After a while I began to wonder: Why do so many foreigners, Americans especially, react so strongly to this place, as though it were specially designed by a neurologist to poke a nerve? A young American writer asked me one day, "How can you not find this place sinister?" Besides watching the country, I began to watch the watchers, hoping to learn how a country so objectively benign (since the war, that is) could seem, to foreigners of great perception and sense, subjectively so "sinister." Partly the war, yes. People sometimes remark that "they," the Japanese, showed in the war "their" potential for volatility and for destruction. I get angry when I hear this, because it is basically rubbish. In the 1930s Japan was under military domination, and it did what military regimes always do, whether in the Far East or in Latin America (think of the Argentines' Falklands adventure) or in the Middle East (Saddam Hussein's invasion and sacking of Kuwait). Army officers rely on conquest to legitimize their rule. They understand guns better than politics, and when confronted with problems, they use the tools they understand. The experience of the 1930s is a cautionary tale about military rule first, and about Japanese culture only secondarily, if at all. Don't blame "national character" or "culture" or other such metaphysical concoctions, I tell people, blame the political system, and try to improve it. However, it is pointless to deny that the war is still alive with us Americans and colors our feelings about Japan, even after these fifty years.

182

This, however, was not the answer. Japan today is if anything too antimilitarist. Many of the foreigners who come here and are frightened or upset are, like the young writer, not old enough to remember the war. They are reacting to the Japan they are seeing *now*. What, then? I think they are reacting to the Japanese traditional values. Liberals have spent the past few hundred years repudiating and, when necessary, rooting out and destroying hierarchic collectivism. And Japan's Platonic side—we should be more forthright about this than we are—is the enemy of the competitive individualism that we stand for and sometimes fight for. When American liberals bump into the preliberal traditional values of Japan, we feel the same way as when we bump into them among American religious fundamentalists. We get the creeps. Our brains may rightly tell us that illiberal values among Christian fundamentalists or Japanese salarymen don't much threaten anybody when they are overlaid with democracy and capitalism and science. Our brains tell us, indeed, that within a liberal system a sprinkling of illiberal values is a source of variety and vitality. But we still get the creeps. We know our old opponent Plato too well to feel at ease when we sense him nearby.

183

Still I was not wholly satisfied. My own experience was that the traditional values are very much alive in Japan, but that today they are mixed in with everything else. They are tiles in the mosaic, but no longer the dominant hue. Something else there is that makes us uneasy—something we are not always honest about. In Japan, so much of ourselves is handed back to us naked and stark, magnified so that we have to look straight at it. We are uncomfortable with the traditional Japanese distinction between *honne* and *tatemae*—between the truth you feel in your heart and the "truth" you utter ritually in public. Yet Donald Richie is right: every society has *honne* and *tatemae*, the Japanese are merely the only ones unhypo-critical enough to have words for them. How many times have we heard American politicians say, "We're going to win tomorrow!" when everybody knows the cause is hopeless? Is that a lie? Is it different from Kochan's "Sorry, no fish today"? Or take the nationalism and tribalism of the Japanese: plainly they believe that to be born Japanese is special, and that people outside the Japanese national family count less. But how many times have our eyes skipped over what my friend from India used to call the Pakistani airplane news, a three-inch newspaper article with a headline like "Jetliner Crashes in Pakistan; No Americans Aboard"? Recently, atop Mount Fuji, there were some incidents in which people running rest stops for hikers proclaimed "Japanese only!" and slammed the door on footsore foreigners. What about my friend in North Carolina who had trouble getting his Toyota worked on because it was foreign? Or the blacks who boycott Korean-American businesses in New York? We are appalled by the mutual back-scratching that goes on between the Japanese monopolies and their government protectors; meanwhile our city councils are busy granting monopoly rights to cable-TV franchises that return the favor in the form of lucrative fees and perks for the city government. We recoil from the conformity we see in the Japanese schools. What about the eight-year-old schoolboy in Texas who in 1990 was isolated from his classmates for months on end because he refused to cut off his little ponytail? We Americans talk up individualism, but could it be that we see more of ourselves in the Japanese corporate mass-man than we quite like to admit? We forget how strongly conformist American society remains—how many people go to law school or business school, start smoking, or wear wing tips just because others do. Real, Emersonian nonconformists, who stand alone, are as rare as ever; our "nonconformists" travel in packs—New Agers, fundamentalists, ethnic clans, whatever.

184

And so around and around I spun, seeing much in Japan that made me uneasy or angry, yet seeing little that, if I thought a bit, I could not remember also having seen at home. At last I came to my present state, in which I am inclined to say that Japan is different, yes, but not *especially* different. And if you say that Japan is unique and always harp on how utterly unlike America it is, I will want to fight the point: not because you may be misunderstanding Japan, but because you will be failing to look our own country in the eye.

185

The Japanese work very hard at making their country better. I had not expected that people in a place that is so averse to public criticism would be so devotedly, sometimes neurotically, *self*-critical. For a century and a half, they have run their country on the working assumption that everything in the West is better or more advanced. The dark side of the legacy is a clinging sense of insecurity that diminishes but does not seem to go away. I talked to a young Japanese diplomat who had grown up in the period of wealth and power and modern attitudes, who had been educated at top universities in Japan and England. Yet even he felt lower in status, somehow smaller and less assured, when talking to an American or European than when talking to an Asian or African. One of Japan's most famous journalists, though thoroughly globalized, told me how struck she is during economic summit meetings by the inevitable group photos of presidents and prime ministers: always they show one unblinkably different face in the midst of the tall white men. You need to know names to tell the French leader from the German leader, but the prime minister of Japan you can always spot at a glance. Yes, I realized, try to imagine how you would feel seeing that one of the people in the pictures is always obviously different and that it is always you. You feel that perhaps you can never fully belong. But there is the other side, too. I had never before met so many people who examined their country so mercilessly for any comparative weaknesses and who were so driven to fix them. The Japanese absolutely cannot abide the thought of being second-rate. Neither, indeed, can the Americans. Yet in Japan I saw precious little of the smugness and complacency that are so common among Americans, especially the patriots.

186

From Japan the Americans look more and more like a bunch of lazy whiners, no longer willing to try their hardest and sacrifice in order to be the best. Within the mantle of exaggeration is, I now think, a molten core of truth. Americans on average still try hard and care about their country. Yet too many people are more interested in scavenging for carrion or gaming the system than in building a better country the old-fashioned way, with sweat. Books with titles like *Wealth Without Risk* are selling rather too well. People believe that they have government benefits coming to them and that the bill for the goodies belongs to someone else, which is why the federal budget deficit fails to go away. Saving is low, investment is low. High-school students do in a week about as much homework as their Japanese counterparts do in a day—they do less studying, even, than Japanese elementary-school students—yet no one seems to expect much better of them. Racially and ethnically organized political groups are busy listing all the perks and positions they are entitled to by dint of being oppressed. Managers pay themselves fat bonuses and seven-figure salaries, while their companies underperform. Labor unions call for protection from foreigners who work too hard for too little. Fathers walk away and families fall apart.

187

I do not mean to exaggerate. The old days were not so different and in many ways, of course, were worse. Moreover, the United States is blessed with what are probably the most adaptable and responsive social institutions in the world. In particular, America is blessed with a political system that was capable of removing a malfeasant president from office peacefully and a scientific system that still beats the competition hollow. Yet I worry, because America's problems today are moral rather than institutional, and moral problems are the hardest kind to fix. Japan's problems are the other way around. I believe I can tell you ways to make the Japanese political system work better; but if you ask me how to make American teenagers care more about studying and less about showing off their Corvettes, I can only shake my head dumbly. I wish you could take the Japanese public, with its willingness to work hard to improve whatever can be improved, and combine it with American social and political institutions, with their flexibility and openness and decency. Then what a country you'd have!

188

I do wish for that, but it cannot be. We will all have to make do with a poor second-best: we will have to continue to rely on the two countries, by nagging westward across the Pacific and competing eastward, to drag each other bumpily in the right direction. True, the Japanese, like everybody else, hate to be criticized. In fact, they hate it more than most, because they tend to view criticism as a sign of enmity. But the truth is that, for all their protests about Japan "bashing," criticism from abroad is of tremendous benefit to them. Foreign criticism is a useful corrective and an invaluable spur to improvement. It is an intellectual market-opener, and a far less dangerous kind of market-opener than foreign threats. Now that Japan is too powerful to rely on having foreigners twist her arm, she must learn to rely instead on having them flail her ideas, an altogether healthier kind of *gaiatsu*. Sooner or later, the Japanese must learn to greet outside criticism with welcome rather than with panic—which is one reason why the criticism ought to continue. Eventually they will learn, and we will remember, that criticism is not the same as violence. Then the pernicious talk that equates criticism with "bashing" will simmer down. And as for the Americans, what is our own best hope? Is there hope that our self-dealing executives and anachronistic unions will rush to reform themselves because it is the smart thing to do? Little or none, as far as I can see. Is there hope that our multitude of special-interest groups—the farm lobby, the business lobby, the affirmative-action lobby, the this lobby and the that lobby—will spontaneously renounce the government pork barrel and shift their energies to self-improvement? Not much. That parents will rise up to demand more homework or a longer school year for their children? We Americans may tell ourselves again and again that the slippage in our standards and in our habits must be reversed, that our hands belong on the plow rather than in our neighbors' pockets; the Japanese tell us, too. But America is too big to be pushed around militarily or, for the most part, diplomatically. The only *gaiatsu* that works on so stubborn and strong a people is steadfast economic competition. We will have it from Japan, and it is our best hope. To Americans, Japan has at last become what America has always been to the Japanese: the unavoidable other, the reality that must be faced, the Outnation, the *gaikoku*.

Part Three

189

I see that in my groping for the elephant I have failed to make sense of it. Pieces, only pieces, butted together clumsily. Perhaps, then, I have done justice to a country. Yet I see that I have left out many pieces, pieces that I will remember.

190

After dark, dinnertime. The little town of Tensui in the hills of Kumamoto prefecture. Mr. Ikemoto, the farmer, is a shortish man, maybe fifty, with big hands that have done work. His foreign houseguest is seated across the dinner table on the tatami-mat floor, dressed in *yukata* (summer kimono, used as a house robe) and trying to keep his folded legs awake, vainly. The Ikemotos have an orange farm, and it brings them a more than comfortable income, although they are worried about the recent liberalization allowing American oranges into the market and, characteristically, their response is to work harder than ever. Their house is rich with the warm woodwork of Japan, and the wide-open, straight-lined traditional design fills the house with air and space. They have set out a meal of tempura and noodles and chicken. Good home cooking after a hot bath. Yet even in this secure place one feels that the glacier, the ancient society, is melting away, and one feels relieved and sad both at once. Mr. Ikemoto is a fifth-generation farmer whose family has been on this land for a hundred years. The older son, Yuichi, who is fifteen, plans to become a hair stylist. The younger, Shumei, wants to work for the prefectural government. The parents tell me the kids haven't made up their minds. One of them might still decide to continue the farm. I turn to the boys, and they are emphatic: no. No farming. I believe them. The line will be broken. Downstairs, I had already noticed, is a traditional Japanese-style squat toilet; upstairs is the Western kind. One for the parents, the other for the kids.

191

Another dinner, this time with four or five middle-aged men. The subject of women comes up. Yes, says one man, my daughters are just like Americans, strong and assertive and practically wearing moustaches. Another man, a few years younger than the others, begins to talk about his wife. She gave up working when their first child was born, fifteen years ago. But she is a woman of intelligence and became more and more frustrated and angry and bored and she took it out on him. Now she has a job grading tests for a correspondence school; she finds her life unfulfilling, empty; she wants a divorce. —I know, says another man, my wife also talks sometimes about divorce, but you know it's just talk to get leverage. Heads nod, but the reply is not what anyone expects. No, says the other man: not for leverage. The divorce is going to happen, I have agreed to it. Our marriage is over. As I listen to him I am seized again with that feeling of the familiar, the too familiar, reaching out from the center of the strange. I feel quite irrationally like the missionary who has brought measles to a pristine continent. My own parents were divorced; half of younger Americans' marriages now end that way. The dinner conversation moves on and I say nothing to this middle-aged man, who smiles bravely. But my heart aches for him and for the price that his country may pay for liberation.

192

Firestorms. Dinnertime again, now in Osaka: Mrs. Tadokoro, my friend's mother, is recalling the war. She was nineteen; the Americans had been bombing Tokyo night after night, pounding and pounding and pounding; people couldn't sleep. On the night of March 9-10, 1945, the Americans incinerated Tokyo with a thousand tons of firebombs, indiscriminately, indeed deliberately, gutting sixteen square miles and killing at least half as many civilians as in Hiroshima. (There were few factories or installations of military significance—

mostly, rather, wooden houses, which went up like tinder-
boxes. It was a terror bombing.) When the sirens sounded,
Mrs. Tadokoro ran to Kinshi-cho Park. As she ran she saw an
electrical pole glow hotter and hotter in the flames and then
crash down. In the park many people, most with suitcases,
waited through the night while around them Tokyo burned.
Of her house, the next morning, nothing remained but some
stones. All this she tells with intelligent eyes but a passive
face: dispassionately. (Shoganai.) Weeks later, I notice that
when Masao Maruyama speaks of the war he allows himself
no sentiment, only precision. He is in his mid-seventies,
has white hair and beakish nose, is generous with his smile,
speaks with an old man's voice but a young man's vigor. He
is recalling August 1945. He and the others in his unit were
gathered in front of the general headquarters building for
morning assembly. It was a bright, clear morning in Ujina,
by the sea, a bit over two miles from the center of Hiroshima. A member of the general staff was giving the morning
talk. Suddenly their eyes were dazzled by something like
lightning, and a sudden wind tore off the general officer's
cap. Everyone plunged into fox holes; from down there he
thought he heard a very loud noise. They climbed out later.
"Something terrible had happened." All the windows of the
concrete headquarters building had been blown out. Behind
the building a very high column of smoke was slowly, slowly
rising; where the top of the smoke column met the flat cloud

above, he saw light playing within. Ten minutes later, people began to pour into the compound from the city, falling to the ground once they were within the gates. They were like ghosts. Many walked as though senseless, with arms held out in front of them. Women were half-naked, their clothes blown to rags. Some people clutched cloths around their bodies like shawls. Some had glass shards embedded in their strewn hair, and blood ran down their faces. Some had living skin falling off their backs. "It was a picture of hell—a picture of hell." Upstairs in the office, the door had been blown off and the tables were turned upside down and the papers scattered by the wind. The one man who had remained inside that morning was sitting with his head already bandaged. They asked if he was all right and all he said was, "We must invent a new bomb." After that he remembers nothing more of that day except a dark sky and eerie rainfall (the so-called "black rain"), and then seeing the flames as Hiroshima burned all that night. He was reminded of the great earthquake of 1923; the sky was bright with fire.

193

English lessons. I am in Nara, along with many boring temples, some fine statuary, and every schoolchild in Japan. The junior-high and high-school students take class trips a whole grade at a time, and on this day in May most of them seem to be in Nara, boys wearing black pants and white shirts, girls in

white sailor blouses and navy-blue skirts. The huge main hall
of Todai-ji and the gigantic cloddish Buddha within being
too dull to hold my attention—they were tourist traps even in
their day (A.D. 752)—I am watching the students instead. The
students are also watching me. They are scouting for *gaijin*, foreigners, to use as homework, and four of them slip under my
radar. As I am mailing a postcard I hear behind me, in barely
recognizable English, a tiny "excuse me," and I spin around to
see a quartet of girls armed with sheets of paper listing English
phrases and Japanese translations. As always in Japan, the oldest,
who is fourteen, takes charge. "What is your name," she reads,
not stopping to comprehend my answer before moving on to
"Where are you going on your sleep"—"trip," I realize, by
reading their cribsheet. They are equipped, I notice, for all
gaijin contingencies. "In school we are very free," their sheet
tells them to observe, "but we must wear uniforms."

194

English lessons, II. The national struggle with English, a fight
to the death, goes on and on, waged with especial brutality on
clothing. T-shirts and sweatshirts spotted in the jabberwocky
country:

EUROPEAN DREAM
WE FIND OUT NEW PERSONAL IN THE
SPACE OF A PART FROM DAILY

NOT DANGEROUS

INFORMATION RELATED

ABILITY TO GETHER

AS MUCH

TRENDY NORTEN COLLECE

THE LAND OF FAIRY, WHERE NO ONE

GETS OLD AND GODLY AND GRARE,

WHERE NO ONE GETS OLD AND CRAFFY AND WISE.

ENSIGN

THEY NOMINATED HIM FOR THE OFFICE, NOMINAL KING:

FLUKY

IF YOU CAN DRAW, YOUR FUTURE IS SECURE

NOW TEST YOUR ART TALENT!

FAMOUS ARTISTS COURSE

U.S CENTURY

SERVICE FREE ESTIMATES

O Japan! Thy mome raths outgrabe!

195

Outsiders. —The bitter European man, middle-aged and missing teeth, sitting at the sushi bar with his Japanese wife and their teenaged girl. He is a classical-ballet choreographer and teacher, invited to come to Japan and teach at a school here some years ago. Now he is sour and angry. The Japanese have their way of doing ballet, and the fact that it is ponderous and mechanical and contrary to the spirit of the art is of no concern to them; trying to suggest other ways merely gets you branded a troublemaker and pushed aside. You must choreograph the way everybody else choreographs or else try to go it alone, setting up your own studio, and in doing this you are met with nothing but indifference and inhospitality and attempts to blacken you. All this he was eager to tell me, this angry man, who perhaps was not so very flexible himself. —The American baseball player, a pitcher recruited out of the University of Illinois to come work for IBM Japan and, not completely coincidentally, to play on their baseball team—corporate baseball being ferociously competitive and very, very serious. Angry at first, then resigned, he has been benched after coming all this way, despite being a winning pitcher: though he is no green eighteen-year-old, he has not paid his dues and waited his turn. Thus the fate of the junior man, however exceptional his circumstances or his ability, in Japan. —"Boss," the owner of El Rancho Grande, in the rolling grassy highlands of Kyushu. He has loved horses since he was twelve. Now his son, a small, homely man of twenty-four who smiles easily and looks fine in leather chaps, is a champion rider, by no means sorry that his father quit Hitachi twenty years ago to open Japan's first American-style dude ranch. The horses, the furniture, the clothing—practically everything comes from America; the boy has been there, now, eight times, he tells me as our horses climb a sunny hill. Later I find Boss, looking like a Texas ranch hand but six inches shorter, building a fence near the stables. We have a conversation, but it is the contentment in the shining eyes that I will remember.

196

I will remember: Sapporo's August festival, an excuse for a sprawling street party in which merchants line the streets with stalls, and young men, wearing *happi*, the traditional festival garb of short shorts and light tunic, carry portable shrines. "Carry," however, does not do justice. The *mikoshi* are very heavy; it takes dozens of men (sometimes joined by women) to carry them; the carriers chant and dance and bounce their load up and down, so that the thick beams supporting it dig into the shoulders and leave, sometimes, red lumps the size of apricots. But this is done for pleasure, the pleasure of enduring and straining together, back bonded to chest by sweat. —Hirosaki's Neputa Matsuri, nighttime festival of floats: each translucent drum-shaped float painted with scenes of angry demons and elegant medieval women and then lit brilliantly from the inside—dozens of them towed down the street by children and adults in long, stately procession, made hypnotic by the steady pounding of big drums and the piping of high flutes, a single obsessive refrain repeated all night. —Tokyo's Shinjuku, the great nightlife district where I arrived one Saturday night utterly unpre-

pared, and emerged from a subway tunnel blinking unbeliev-
ingly at the oz of flashing three-story neon and the dense
crowds of teenagers and young adults, more than I had ever
seen on the street before, all with the high-powered haircuts
and up-to-date smart clothing that have become indispens-
able in Tokyo.

197

I will remember the skins of Japan. Mountain skins: I am
fitfully dozing on the bullet-train near Sendai, and start
awake. I turn to look out the window, and there are the hills
staring back at me, glowing in the evening sun. All at once
I want nothing more than to touch those hills—I want this
overwhelmingly. Like all the Japanese hills, they are steep
but roll gently, with none of the cragginess I'm used to
from home; and, like all the Japanese hills and most of the
mountains, they are densely verdant from base to top, everywhere—so densely lush that from a distance they look like
nubby green-black velvet, as though these mountains are soft
to the core. Sometimes riding over them in a cable lift (Japan
is full of cable lifts—the tourists adore them), I feel that if I
were to step outside and fall, the mountain skin would catch
me softly, and then I could burrow through the covering of
trees till safely reaching the ground below. Odd, I think:
the hills and mountains of Japan grow more intimate with
distance—softer to the touch.

198

And the skin of the Japanese themselves: this especially I will remember. I had heard about it. Donald Richie, writing in *The Inland Sea*: "Perhaps nowhere on earth is there more beautiful skin than in Japan. Usually hairless, it is not a mere covering. It is as though the entire body, all the way through, were composed of this soft, smooth lustrousness." But still I had not imagined how the silky, nut-brown skin stretched vibrant over the frame. By comparison my skin looks big-pored, pasty, rough, as though the sculptor had neglected the final buffing and smoothing that he gave the Japanese. On the subway sometimes it was all I could do not to reach over and stroke the skin of the person sitting next to me—just as, indeed, Japanese women sometimes stroke the hair of blonds.

199

I will remember scenes in darkness. Sumida Park, across the river from the fashionable parts of Tokyo; it is long after dark, and deep in a glade where I can hardly see to walk I am being given a guided tour of Japanese outdoor sex, which as near as I can tell looks just like non-Japanese outdoor sex. So much for Japanese uniqueness. We are all of us pathetic adventurers, scrounging like mice for little triumphs. —Kamakura, an hour from Tokyo by train, an ancient capital of Japan; finding a gate open, I have wandered for the first time into the grounds of the Kencho-ji temple, built in the mid-thirteenth century but, despite its antiquity and like all the temples I saw in Japan, wholly unmysterious by day. Now, however, it is night, and I make my way up the path unsure what is ahead and wondering whether by now a caretaker will have locked me in. All at once the trees part, and I am looking up at the temple gate, topheavily made in 1754 of many tons of wood, standing almost black against the dark blue sky, lit only by the dim glare of a Coke machine and a street light some distance away. It is, at this moment, a projection of the earth itself, perhaps 250 years old or 250 million, and it makes me solemn and afraid. (Later I went back to see the temple by day, and of course I was disappointed.) —Shinbashi, in downtown Tokyo, long after supper. I am on the bus, sitting in the shadows by a window, staring sadly at my feet. After a farewell dinner in my favorite basement restaurant, where we debated whether raw squid tastes like rubber eraser (it does), amiable Nakahara and bright-eyed Sasaki have pressed a hundred yen into my palm and put me on the bus home. They are waving good-bye from the curb, smiling broadly. As the bus pulls away, the Tokyo night enfolds them and closes up, leaving no trace of my insertion.

200

I will remember this, too: —Tokyo. A hot July day downtown in the city, across the street from Hibiya Park, whose trees are ringing with the racket of cicadas. Like everyone else I am pushing ahead, businesslike and sweaty in my suit and tie. The sidewalk is crowded, especially here, near the Imperial Hotel, a faceless monster built on the site where Frank Lloyd Wright's infinitely more interesting Imperial stood until it was, characteristically, deemed too small and razed. Out of the corner of my eye I notice a white-shirted businessman walking in my direction across a corporate cobblestone plaza—walking not toward me, however, but toward, of all things, one of a few manicured trees in a planter. As I slow down to watch him, he puts his right hand on the tree trunk and uncups it, and there deposits a living cicada. It is big and ugly, of the sort that makes many of the trees in Tokyo sound like jigsaws. Why did he do it? Long before I have time to finish wondering, he has walked on toward his business. And I walked on toward mine. Yet I will remember this moment, I believe, indefinitely. Do not ask me why. I could tell you only that at that instant, I know, I touched the elephant.

CPSIA information can be obtained
at www.ICGtesting.com
Printed in the USA
LVHW021123221221
706919LV00003B/113

9 781949 450033